Also Published in English

STORY UNDER FULL SAIL
ANTI-WORLDS AND THE FIFTH ACE

Translated by

ROBERT BLY

GUY DANIELS

VERA DUNHAM

LAWRENCE FERLINGHETTI

ALLEN GINSBERG

MAX HAYWARD

STANLEY KUNITZ

LOUIS SIMPSON

WILLIAM JAY SMITH

H. W. TJALSMA

RICHARD WILBUR

and others

Andrei Voznesensky

NOSTALGIA FOR THE PRESENT

Edited by
Vera Dunham and Max Hayward

With Forewords by
Edward M. Kennedy and Arthur Miller

DOUBLEDAY & COMPANY, INC., GARDEN CITY, NEW YORK 1978

Library of Congress Cataloging in Publication Data

Voznesenskiĭ, Andreĭ Andreevich.
Nostalgia for the present.

I. Dunham, Vera S., 1912–   II. Hayward, Max.
III. Title.
PG3489.4.Z6A223   891.7′1′44
ISBN: 0-385-08368-8 (hardcover)
0-385-08373-4 (paperback)
Library of Congress Catalog Card Number 72–76218

ACKNOWLEDGMENTS

Phone Booth and *An Arrow in the Wall,* translated by Richard Wilbur, first appeared in *The Mind-Reader* by Richard Wilbur, published by Harcourt Brace Jovanovich, Inc., and is here reprinted by permission of the author, copyright © 1976 by Richard Wilbur.

Dogalypse, translated by Lawrence Ferlinghetti, Maureen Sager, Catherine Leach, and Vera Dunham, *American Buttons,* translated by Lawrence Ferlinghetti, and *Breath Donor,* translated by Lawrence Ferlinghetti, reprinted by permission of City Lights Books, copyright © 1972.

Nostalgia for the Present, translated by Vera Dunham and H. W. Tjalsma, and *Do Not Forget,* translated by William Jay Smith and Vera Dunham, reprinted by permission of *Saturday Review.* They first appeared in the February 4, 1978, issue of *Saturday Review.*

Winter at the Track, translated by William Jay Smith and Max Hayward, and *Striptease on Strike,* translated by Max Hayward, reprinted by permission of Max Hayward. Copyright © 1967 by Max Hayward.

*An Ironical Elegy Born in Those Most Distressing Moments When . . .
One Cannot Write,* translated by William Jay Smith and Nicholas Fersen, *June '68,* translated by William Jay Smith and Nicholas Fersen, and *Ice Block,* translated by William Jay Smith and Vera Dunham, reprinted by permission of *The New Republic.*

FOREWORDS

I had the pleasure of meeting Andrei Voznesensky on a visit I made to the Soviet Union in 1974. He was generous enough to invite me to his home in Moscow, where I spent a very delightful evening.

I was with him again in October 1977, at a reading he gave at the Library of Congress in Washington. The occasion was a chance for me not only to join in a significant public honor in our nation's capital to one of the world's greatest living poets, but also to renew a private friendship that has had special meaning for me and my family. One of the poems which he read that night, and which is included in the present volume, is a poem about my brother Bob.

In the swirl of immediate and pressing issues and concerns, we sometimes tend to overlook the larger qualities that give meaning and hope to life, the eternal shared values that are at the heart of civilization and that give direction to the lives of our own citizens and to those of many different lands.

Poets give us grace. With their special gifts of perception and expression, they help us to lift our feet from the dusty road, to keep our eyes on the horizon, to deal in a more understanding way with the experience of life.

Walt Whitman wrote that "the proof of a poet is that his country absorbs him as affectionately as he has absorbed it."

President Kennedy, in honoring Robert Frost at Amherst College in October 1963, said:

We must never forget that art is not a form of propaganda; it is a form of truth. When power leads us toward arrogance, poetry reminds us of our limitations. When power narrows the areas of our concern, poetry reminds us of the richness and diversity of our existence. When power corrupts, poetry cleanses.

And of Voznesensky himself, America's own great poet Robert Lowell once wrote:

> Voznesensky is full of invention, fireworks, and humor, but he is always writing about awkward, anguished things: hunting a hare, a girl in a freezing telephone booth, the invasion of Russia, departure from a friend. He writes about buildings, the New York airport, the Paris flea market, the days of Stalin, striptease girls, and Tolstoy. Frequently, he has the steady sorrowing sympathy of Pasternak and Chekhov.

Volumes like this one help us to understand the central place of the arts and humanities in our lives. We can build bridges of friendship and co-operation between the people of the United States and the people of the Soviet Union. Whatever the passions of the moment that may divide us on various issues of foreign policy, we know that by increasing our understanding of one another we reduce our conflicts and divisions. We gain new confidence that creation will prevail over destruction, that hope will prevail over fear, that knowledge will prevail over ignorance.

The ultimate challenge for our two strong nations is what we can do together for humanity, what we can do together to improve the lives of all peoples on this earth. There is an old Russian proverb that describes Soviet-American relations: it says, "A mountain and a mountain cannot meet, but individual human beings can come together." It is in that spirit that I welcome this new collection of Andrei Voznesensky's poems.

Senator Edward M. Kennedy

I was much surprised when in the early sixties a group of Soviet poets suddenly appeared reading their poems to tens of thousands of people in football stadiums and big theaters, the more surprising when their poems were very good indeed. Their poems, many of them, cut close to the bone on sensitive public issues. In fact, the poet alone seems to have been allowed a license which is not shared by novelist, playwright, or any other public artist or interpreter. This is so completely at odds with our tradition that one does not know how to comprehend it. I have wondered whether way back in time, in Russia, there was not some religious exemption, some aspect of holiness which the poet was thought to possess, quite as though he were some sort of subconscious connection with the soul of the race.

Voznesensky comes to us not only as a marvelously lyrical poet; he is also a star whose name and face and work would be familiar to enormous numbers of people in Russia. And so, too, his poems in this new collection are not, I think, only attempts to create beautiful forms of language addressed to his peers. He has tried to speak, in these poems, as though he alone had a tongue, as though he alone had somehow learned the news of today and tomorrow, as though the space taken up by his poem were precious and must not be used by counterfeit words. He has carved out a private speech for public occasions, an intimacy which is yet open-armed toward the world.

Arthur Miller

СОДЕРЖАНИЕ

I

CONTENTS

II

xvi

III

IV

V

LIST OF ILLUSTRATIONS
(Illustrations follow page 93)

PART I

НОСТАЛЬГИЯ ПО НАСТОЯЩЕМУ

Я не знаю, как остальные,
но я чувствую жесточайшую
не по прошлому ностальгию —
ностальгию по настоящему.

Будто послушник хочет к Господу,
ну а доступ лишь к настоятелю —
так и я умоляю доступа
без посредников к настоящему.

Будто сделал я что-то чуждое,
или даже не я — другие.
Упаду на поляну — чувствую
по живой земле ностальгию.

Нас с тобой никто не расколет,
но когда тебя обнимаю —
обнимаю с такой тоскою,
будто кто тебя отнимает.

Когда слышу тирады подленькие
оступившегося товарища,
я ищу не подобья — подлинника,
по нему грущу, настоящему.

Одиночества не искупит
в сад распахнутая столярка.
Я тоскую не по искусству,
задыхаюсь по-настоящему.

И когда мне хохочет в рожу
идиотствующая мафия,
говорю: «Идиоты — в прошлом.
В настоящем — рост понимания».

NOSTALGIA FOR THE PRESENT

I don't know about the rest of you,
but I feel the cruelest
nostalgia—not for the past—
but nostalgia for the present.

A novice desires to approach the Lord
but is permitted to do so only by her Superior.
I beg to be joined, without intermediary,
to the present.

It's as if I had done something wrong,
Not I even—but others.
I fall down in a field and feel
nostalgia for the living earth.

No one can ever tear you away,
and yet when I embrace you again
I feel overcome by terrible pain
as if you were being stolen from me.

When I hear the nasty tirades
of a friend who has taken a false step,
I don't look for what he seems to be,
I grieve for what he really is.

A window opening on a garden
will not redeem loneliness.
I long not for art—I choke
on my craving for reality.

And when the Mafia laughs in my face
idiotically, I say:
"Idiots are all in the past. The present
calls for fuller understanding."

Хлещет черная вода из крана.
хлещет ржавая настоявшаяся,
хлещет красная вода из крана,
я дождусь — пойдет настоящая.

Что прошло, то прошло. К лучшему.
Но прикусываю как тайну
ностальгию по настающему,
что настанет. Да не застану.

Black water spurts from the faucet,
Brackish water, stale water,
rusty water flows from the faucet—I'll wait
for the real water to come.

Whatever is past is past. So much the better.
But I bite at it as at a mystery,
nostalgia for the impending
present.
      And I'll never catch hold of it.

(translated by Vera Dunham and H. W. Tjalsma)

ЧАСТНОЕ КЛАДБИЩЕ

Памяти Роберта Лоуэлла

Ты проходил в переделкинскую калитку —
голову набок, щекою прижавшись к плечу —
как прижимал недоступную зрению скрипку.
Скрипка пропала. Слушать хочу.

В домик Петра ты входил близоруко.
Там есть в двух метрах зарубка, как от топора.
Стал ты примериться под зарубку —
встал в пустоту, что осталась от роста Петра.

Ах, как звенит пустота вместо бывшего тела!
Новая тень под зарубкой стоит.
Чаща над кладбищем облетела.
И недоступная скрипка кричит.

В чаще затеряно частное кладбище.
Мать и отец твои. Где же здесь ты?
Будто из книги вынули вкладыши,
и невозможно страницу найти.

Как тебе, Роберт, в новой пустыне?
Частное кладбище носим в себе.
Пестик тоски в мировой пустоте,
мчащийся мимо, как тебе имя?
Прежнее имя, как платье, лежит на плите.

Вот ты и вырвался из лабиринта.
Что тебе, тень, под зарубкой в избе?
Я принесу пастернаковскую рябину.
Но и она не поможет тебе.

FAMILY GRAVEYARD

To the memory of Robert Lowell

At Peredelkino you passed through the gate,
Your head to one side, your cheek on your shoulder tight
As on a violin held somehow out of sight;
I listen now, but it is there no more.

In Moscow, near-sighted, you entered Peter's hut,
Examining a notch some six feet from the floor
Hacked as by an ax; you stood below that notch
And measured yourself against Great Peter's height.

Once filled by a body, how the void resounds!
Beneath the notch a new ghost fills the air;
The maples in the graveyard now are bare;
And through the dark the violin thinly sounds.

The family graves lie deep within the wood:
Your parents both are there, but where in the dark are you?
The bookmarks in the book have been removed,
One cannot find the page as one leafs through.

How is it, Robert, there in your wild land?
Within us we all bear our family graves;
How can we name the heart of sorrow's flower
As it races past us through dark cosmic waves?
Here on the stone the name that you once had rests like discarded
                clothes.

So through the labyrinth you've made your way?
And yet beneath that notch I still hear you,
And bring these berries from Pasternak's rowan tree
For all the good that rowanberries do.

     (translated by William Jay Smith and Fred Starr)

7

С А Г А

Ты меня на рассвете разбудишь,
проводить необутая выйдешь.
Ты меня никогда не забудешь.
Ты меня никогда не увидишь.

Заслонивши тебя от простуды,
я подумаю: «Боже всевышний!
Я тебя никогда не забуду
и уже никогда не увижу».

Эту реку в мурашках запруды,
это Адмиралтейство и Биржу
я уже никогда не забуду
и уже никогда не увижу.

Не мигают, слезятся от ветра
безнадежные карие вишни.
Возвращаться — плохая примета.
Я тебя никогда не увижу.

Даже если на землю вернемся
мы вторично, согласно Гафизу,
мы конечно с тобой разминемся.
Я тебя никогда не увижу.

И окажется так минимальным
наше непониманье с тобою
перед будущим непониманьем
двух живых с пустотой неживою!

И качнутся бессмысленной высью
пара фраз долетевших отсюда:
«Я тебя никогда не забуду».
«Я тебя никогда не увижу».

SAGA

You will awaken me at dawn
And barefoot lead me to the door;
You'll not forget me when I'm gone,
You will not see me any more.

Lord, I think, in shielding you
From the cold wind of the open door:
I'll not forget you when I'm gone,
I shall not see you any more.

The Admiralty, the Stock Exchange
I'll not forget when I am gone.
I'll not see Leningrad again,
Its water shivering at dawn.

From withered cherries as they turn,
Brown in the wind, let cold tears pour:
It's bad luck always to return,
I shall not see you any more.

And if what Hafiz says is true
And we return to earth once more,
We'll miss each other if it's true;
I shall not see you any more.

Our quarrels then will fade away
To nothing when we both are gone,
And when one day our two lives clash
Against that void to which they're drawn.

Two silly phrases rise to sway
On heights of madness from earth's floor:
I'll not forget you when I'm gone,
I shall not see you any more.

(translated by William Jay Smith and Vera Dunham)

ПРАВИЛА ПОВЕДЕНИЯ ЗА СТОЛОМ

Уважьте пальцы пирогом,
в солонку курицу макая,
но умоляю об одном —
не трожьте музыку руками!

Нашарьте огурец со дна
и стан справасидящей дамы,
даже под током провода —
но музыку нельзя руками.

Она с душою наравне.
Берите трешницы с рублями,
но даже вымытыми не
хватайте музыку руками.

И прогрессист и супостат,
мы материалисты с вами,
но музыка — иной субстант,
где не губами, а устами...

Руками ешьте даже суп,
но с музыкой — беда такая!
Чтоб вам не оторвало рук,
не трожьте музыку руками.

TABLE MANNERS

Eat pie with your fingers,
dip your chicken in the salt,
but I ask just one thing of you:
Keep your hands off music.

Grope for a pickle at the bottom
of the jar, and for the bottom
of the lady seated at your right,
but don't grope for music.

Music is on a par with the soul.
Grab rubles and dollars,
but even if your hands are clean,
don't grab music.

Liberal or reactionary,
we are all materialists.
But music is another matter,
to be touched with the heart, not the tongue.

Eat soup with your hands if you like,
but not music—please—
or your hands will be torn off.
Don't touch music with your hands.

(translated by William Jay Smith and Vera Dunham)

1971

ВАСИЛЬКИ ШАГАЛА

Лик ваш серебряный, как алебарда.
Жесты легки.
В вашей гостинице аляповатой
в банке спрессованы васильки.

Милый, вот что вы действительно любите!
С Витебска ими раним и любим.
Дикорастущие сорные тюбики
с дьявольски
     выдавленным
       голубым!

Сирый цветок из породы репейников,
но его синий не знает соперников.
Марка Шагала, загадка Шагала —
рупь у Савеловского вокзала!

Это росло у Бориса и Глеба,
в хохоте нэпа и чебурек.
Во поле хлеба — чуточку неба.
Небом единым жив человек.

В небе коровы парят и ундины.
Зонтик раскройте, идя на проспект.
Родины разны, но небо едино
Небом единым жив человек.

Как занесло васильковое семя
на Елисейские, на поля?
Как заплетали венок Вы на темя
Гранд Опера, Гранд Опера!

В век ширпотреба нет его, неба.
Доля художников хуже калек.
Давать им сребреники нелепо —
небом единым жив человек.

CHAGALL'S CORNFLOWERS

Your face is all of silver like a halberd,
your gestures light.
In your vulgar hotel room
you keep pressed cornflowers.

Dear friend, so this is what you truly love!
Since Vitebsk, cornflowers have wounded
and loved you—those wildflower tubes
of squeezed-out
                    devilish
                              sky-blue.

An orphaned flower of the burdock family,
its blue has no rival.
The mark of Chagall, the enigma of Chagall—
a tattered ruble note at a remote Moscow station.

It grew around St. Boris and St. Gleb,
around guffawing speculators with their greasy fingers.
In a field of grain, add a patch of sky.
Man lives by sky alone.

Cows and water nymphs soar in the sky.
Open your umbrella as you go out on the street.
Countries are many, the sky is one.
Man lives by sky alone.

How did a cornflower seed chance to fall
on the Champs-Elysées, on those fields?
What a glorious garland you wove
for the Paris Opéra.

In the age of consumer goods there is no sky.
The lot of the artist is worse than a cripple's.
Giving him pieces of silver is silly—
man lives by sky alone.

Ваши холсты из фашистского бреда
от изуверов свершали побег.
Свернуто в трубку запретное небо,
но только небом жив человек.

Не протрубили трубы Господни
над катастрофою мировой —
в трубочку свернутые полотна
воют архангельскою трубой!

Кто целовал твое поле, Россия,
пока не выступят васильки?
Твои сорняки всемирно красивы,
хоть экспортируй их, сорняки.

С поезда выйдешь — как окликают!
По полю дрожь.
Поле пришпорено васильками,
как ни уходишь — все не уйдешь...

Выйдешь ли вечером — будто захварываешь,
во поле углические зрачки.
Ах, Марк Захарович, Марк Захарович,
все васильки, все васильки...

Не Иегова, не Иисусе,
ах, Марк Захарович, нарисуйте
непобедимо синий завет —
Небом Единым Жив Человек.

1973

Your canvases made their escape
from the fascist nightmare, from murder,
the forbidden sky rolled up in a tube,
but man lives by sky alone.

While God failed to trumpet
over the horror,
your canvases rolled up in a tube
still howl like Gabriel's horn.

Who kissed your fields, Russia,
until cornflowers bloomed?
Your weeds become glorious in other countries,
you ought to export them.

How they hail you, when you leave the train.
The fields tremble.
The fields are studded with cornflowers.
You can't get away from them.

When you go out in the evening—you seem ill.
Eyes of the unjustly condemned stare from the field.
Ah, Marc Zakharovich, Marc Zakharovich,
is it all the fault of those cornflowers?

Let not Jehovah or Jesus
but you, Marc Zakharovich, paint a testament
of invincible blue—
Man Lives by Sky Alone.

(translated by Vera Dunham and H. W. Tjalsma)

1973

15

* * *

Суздальская Богоматерь,
сияющая на белой стене,
    как кинокассирша
        в полукруглом овале окошечка!
Дай мне
билет,
куда не допускают
после шестнадцати...

O SUZDAL MOTHER OF GOD

O Suzdal Mother of God,
shining on the white wall,
    like that lady cashier
    in her oval ticket window,

provide me a ticket
to that movie
    that can only be seen
    by those under sixteen.

(translated by William Jay Smith and Vera Dunham)

ПРОВИНЦИАЛЬНАЯ ХРОНИКА

Мы с другом шли. За вывескою «Хлеб»
ущелье дуло, как депо судеб.

Нас обступал сиропный городок.
Местный вампир у донорского пункта
на бампере клиентов ждал попутных.

Мой друг хромал. И пузыри земли,
я уточнил бы — пузыри асфальта —
нам попадаясь, клянчили на банку.

«Ты помнишь Анечку-официантку?»

Я помнил. Удивленная лазурь
ее меж подавальщиц отличала.
Носила косу. Говорят, свою.
Когда б не глаз цыганские фиалки
ее бы мог писать Венецианов.
Спешила к сыну с сумками, полна
такою темно-золотою силой,
что женщины при приближеньи Аньки
мужей хватали, как при крике: «Танки!»

Но иногда на зов «Официантка!»
она душою оцепеневала,
и встрепенувшись, шла: «Спешу! Спешу!»

Я помнил Анечку-официантку,
что не меня, а друга целовала
и в деревянном домике жила.
Спешила вечно к сыну. Сын однажды
ее встречал. На нас комплексовал.
К ней, как вьюнок белесый, присосался,
Потом из кухни в зеркало следил
и делал вид, что учит Песни Данте.

PROVINCIAL SCENE

While wind swept down the gorge as from the depot of the fates
I walked with my friend the quiet little streets
below a bakery sign in a sweet southern town.
Beside a blood bank a local vampire
leaned on the bumper of his car, awaiting clients.
My friend limped along, and bubbles from the earth
(or rather, bubbles rising between chinks
in the asphalt) came toward us like bums cadging drinks. . . .

"You remember Annie, the little waitress, don't you?"

I did, of course. It was the astonished blue
of her eyes that distinguished her from her fellow hash-slingers.
She wore a braid, thought to be her own.
Had it not been for the gypsy violet of
her eyes, she might have modeled for Venetsianov.
She was always hurrying to her son with shopping bags of food.
Filled with such dark, golden strength
that any woman who saw her would grab her husband and
disappear
as if someone had cried, "Look out, the tanks are here!"

Often when customers shouted, "Miss!"
her soul would freeze as if she mistook this
for some other signal, and then, waking up, would reply, "I'm
coming, coming."

I remembered her clearly,
little Annie, the waitress—
she had slept with my friend, but not with me—
lived in a shack,
always hurrying to her son. Once the son
stood waiting, felt uneasy with us,
and clung to her like a pale vine; then he
kept watching us in the mirror
while pretending to study his Dante.

19

«Ты помнишь Анечку-официантку?
Ее убил из-за валюты сын.
Одна коса от Анечки осталась».

Так вот куда ты, милая, спешила...

«Он бил ее в постели молотком.
вьюночек, малолетний сутенер, —
у друга на ветру блеснули зубы. —
Ее ассенизаторы нашли,
ее нога отсасывать мешала.
Был труп утоплен в яме выгребной,
как грешница в аду. Старик, Шекспир...»

Она летела над ночной землей.
Она кричала: «Мальчик потерялся!»
Заглядывала форточкой в дома —
«Невинен он, — кричала, — я сама
ударилась! Сметана в холодильнике.
Проголодался? Мальчика не вижу!»
И безнадежно отжимала жижу.

И с круглым люком мерзкая доска
скользила нимбом, как доска иконы.
Нет низкого для Божьей чистоты!

«Ее пришел весь город хоронить.
Гадали — кто? Его подозревали.
Ему сказали: «Поцелуй хоть мать».
Он отказался. Тут и раскололи.
Он не назвал сообщников, дебил».
Сказал я другу: «Это ты убил».

Ты утонула в наших головах
меж новостей и скучных анекдотов.
Не существует рая или ада.
Ты стала мыслью. Кто же ты теперь
в той новой, ирреальной иерархии —

"You remember Annie, the little waitress? She's dead,
  killed by her son for her money;
  all that was left was her false braid."

So that is where you were hurrying, Annie.

"He beat her with a hammer while she slept,
  the little clinging vine, the teen-age pimp."
My friend's teeth glittered in the wind.
"She was found by the sanitation crew
  when her leg blocked their pump.
  Her corpse was stuffed down the outhouse hole—
  like in Shakespeare, bud, like a sinner in hell."

Over the night earth I saw her fly,
  and "I've lost my boy!" I heard her cry
  as she gazed in at the windows.
"He is not guilty!" I heard her scream.
"I hit myself with the hammer!
  In the icebox there is sour cream.
  Aren't you hungry, honey? I can't see my boy . . ."
and she tried to wipe away the excrement. . . .

But the vile board surrounded her all the while
like the hatch of a conning tower or the nimbus of an icon:
In God's eyes nothing is vile.

"The whole town came to her funeral.
  They guessed who'd done it. Suspecting him,
  they said: 'Kiss your mother';
  he refused.
  And it was then that they found him out.
  But he would not say who his accomplices had been."
"You were the killer!" I said to my friend.

Yes, Annie, you drowned in our minds
  between news reports and dirty jokes . . .
  heaven and hell do not exist—
  you drift somewhere in between. Who are you now
  in your new hierarchy?

21

клочок Ничто? тычиночка тоски?
приливы беспокойства пред туманом?
Куда спешишь, гонимая причиной,
необъяснимой нам? зовешь куда?

Прости, что без нужды тебя тревожу.
В том океане, где отсчета нет,
ты вряд ли помнишь 30-40 лет,
субстанцию людей провинциальных
и на кольце свои инициалы?
Но вдруг ты смутно помнишь зовы эти
и на мгновенье оцепеневаешь,
расслышав фразу на одной планете:

«Ты помнишь Анечку-официантку?»

Гуляет ветер судеб, судебный ветер.

A little scrap of nothing, are you? Stamen dusted with grief,
the rush of anxiety that comes before fog descends. . . .
Where are you hurrying now, driven by what we do not know;
where in the world do you want us to go?

Sorry to disturb you for no reason.
Now in that ocean where one can't begin to count,
you have no doubt forgotten your thirty or forty years,
the fabric of provincial people, the initials in your ring.
But maybe you dimly remember their calls,
and for one second your soul may freeze,
catching a phrase that from a planet will descend.

"You remember Annie, the little waitress, don't you?"

The wind of judgment blows, the fateful wind.

                                    (translated by William Jay Smith)

ПОХОРОНЫ ГОГОЛЯ НИКОЛАЯ ВАСИЛЬИЧА

> 1. Завещаю тела моего не погребать
> до тех пор, пока не покажутся явные
> признаки разложения. Упоминаю об
> этом потому, что уже во время самой
> болезни находили на меня минуты
> жизненного опомения, сердце и пульс
> переставали биться...
>
> *Н. В. Гоголь. (Завещание)*

I

Вы живого несли по стране!
Гоголь был в летаргическом сне.
Гоголь думал в гробу на спине:

Разве я некрофил? Это вы!
Любят похороны витии,
поминают, когда мертвы,
забывая, пока живые.

Вы вокруг меня встали в кольцо,
наблюдая, с какою кручиной
погружается нос мой в лицо,
точно лезвие в нож перочинный.

II

«Поднимите мне веки, соотечественники мои,
в летаргическом веке
пробудитесь от галиматьи.
Поднимите мне веки!
Разбуди меня, люд молодой,
мои книги читавший под партой,
потрудитесь понять, что со мной.
Нет, отходят попарно!

THE INTERMENT OF
NIKOLAI VASILICH GOGOL

I direct that my body not be buried until such time as it shows signs of decomposition. I mention this because during my illness there have already been moments of deathly numbness when my heart and pulse stopped beating.

> N. V. Gogol, *Last Will and Testament*

I

You carried him alive through the country,
Gogol in a deep sleep.
Gogol lay in his coffin thinking:

"I'm not necrophiliac; you are.
Russia loves funerals. Forgetting the living,
it prays for you
when you're dead.

"You've gathered in a circle
around me. With such agony
my nose like the blade of a penknife
sinks deeply into my face.

II

"Raise my eyelids, my compatriots,
in our lethargic age
wake up from gibberish.
Raise my eyelids!
Young people who read my books
under your school desks, wake me up.
Try to understand what I'm about.
No, they are going away, two by two!

Грешный дух бронирован в плоть,
безучастную, как каменья.
Помоги мне подняться, Господь,
чтоб упасть пред тобой на колени».

III

«Из-под фрака украли исподнее.
Дует в щель. Но в нее не просунуться.
Что там муки Господние
перед тем, как в могиле проснуться!»
Крик подземный глубин не потряс.
Двое выпили на могиле.
Любят похороны, дивясь,
детвора и чиновничий класс,
как вы любите слушать рассказ,
как Гоголя хоронили.

Вскройте гроб и застыньте в снегу
Гоголь, скорчась, лежит на боку.
Вросший ноготь подкладку прорвал сапогу.

1973-74

My sinful spirit is clad in flesh,
indifferent as stone.
Help me arise, Lord, so I may
fall on my knees before Thee.

III

"They've stolen my linen from under my frock coat.
There's a draft through a crack. But there's no way to get
                                                    through it.
Even Christ suffered less
before waking up in the grave!"
The subterranean cry did not shake the depths.
Two men had a drink on the grave.
We enjoy funerals just as
you enjoy hearing how Gogol was buried.

Unseal his coffin freezing in the snow.
Gogol, writhing, lies on his side.
His twisted toenail has torn the lining in his boot.

(translated by Vera Dunham and H. W. Tjalsma)

1973–74

АВТОМАТ

Москвою кто-то бродит,
накрутит номер мой.
Послушает и бросит —
отбой...

Чего вам? Рифм кило?
Автографа в альбом?
Алло!..
Отбой...

Кого-то повело
в естественный отбор!
Алло!..
Отбой...

А может, ангел в кабеле,
пришедший за душой?
Мы некоммуникабельны.
Отбой...

А может, это совесть,
потерянная мной?
И позабыла голос?
Отбой...

Стоишь в метро конечной
с открытой головой,
и в диске, как в колечке,
замерзнул пальчик твой.

А за окошком мелочью
стучит толпа отчаянная,
как очередь в примерочную
колечек обручальных.

PHONE BOOTH

Someone is loose in Moscow who won't stop
Ringing my phone.
Whoever-it-is listens, then hangs up.
Dial tone.

What do you want? A bushel of rhymes or so?
An autograph? A bone?
Hello?
Dial tone.

Someone's lucky number, for all I know,
Is the same, worse luck, as my own.
Hello!
Dial tone.

Or perhaps it's an angel calling collect
To invite me to God's throne.
Damn, I've been disconnected.
Dial tone.

Or is it my old conscience, my power of choice
To which I've grown
A stranger, and which no longer knows my voice?
Dial tone.

Are you standing there in some subway station, stiff
And hatless in the cold,
With your finger stuck in the dial as if
In a ring of gold?

And is there, outside the booth, a desperate throng
Tapping its coins on the glass, chafing its hands,
Like a line of people who have been waiting long
To be measured for wedding-bands?

Ты дунешь в трубку дальнюю,
и мой воротничок
от твоего дыхания
забьется, как флажок...

Что, мой глухонемой?
Отбой...

Порвалась связь планеты.
Аукать устаю.
Вопросы без ответов.
Ответы в пустоту.

Свело. Свело. Свело.
С тобой. С тобой. С тобой.
Алло. Алло. Алло.
Отбой. Отбой. Отбой.

1974

I hear you breathe and blow into some remote
Mouthpiece, and as you exhale
The lapels of my coat
Flutter like pennants in a gale.

Speak up, friend! Are you deaf and dumb as a stone?
Dial tone.

The planet's communications are broken.
I'm tired of saying *hello*.
My questions might as well be unspoken.
Into the void my answers go.

Thrown together, together
With you, with you unknown.
Hello. Hello. Hello there.
Dial tone. Dial tone. Dial tone.

(translated by Richard Wilbur)

1974

СТРЕЛА В СТЕНЕ

Тамбовский волк тебе товарищ
и друг,
когда ты со стены срываешь
подаренный пенджабский лук!

Как в ГУМе отмеряют ситец,
с плеча откинется рука,
стрела задышит, не насытясь,
как продолжение соска.

С какою женственностью лютой
в стене засажена стрела —
в чужие стены и уюты.
Как в этом женщина была!

Стрела — в стене каркасной стройки,
во всем, что в силе и в цене.
Вы думали — век электроники?
Стрела в стене!

Горите, судьбы и державы!
Стрела в стене.
Тебе от слез не удержаться
наедине, наедине.

Над украшательскими нишами,
как шах семье,
ультиматумативно нищая
стрела в стене!

Шахуй, оторва белокурая!
И я скажу:
«У, олимпийка!» И подумаю:
«Как сжались ямочки в тазу».

AN ARROW IN THE WALL

You'd look right with a wolf from Tambov
For sidekick and friend,
As you tear my Punjabi bow
Down from the wall, and bend it.

Your hand pulls back from the shoulder
As if measuring cloth by the yard;
The arrow pants, and is eager,
Like a nipple extended and hard.

And now, with what feminine fury,
Into the wall it goes—
All the walls of the snug and secure.
There's a woman in that, God knows!

In towers of skeletal steel, —an arrow!
In pomposities one and all.
Who says it's the electronic era?
There's an arrow in the wall!

Burn, privilege and power!
There's an arrow in the wall.
Soon, in a drained and lonely hour,
Your tears will fall.

But dark now, doubly dark,
Over rich embrasures which crawl
With elaborate moldings, your stark
Arrow is in the wall!

All right, you cheeky blonde,
Checkmate me, and I'll say
"Oh, you Olympian!," thinking fondly
Of how your belly-dimples play.

33

«Агрессорка, — добавлю, — скифка...»
Ты скажешь: «Фиг-то»...

Отдай, тетивка сыромятная,
наитишайшую из стрел
так тихо и невероятно,
как тайный ангел отлетел.

На людях мы едва знакомы,
но это тянется года.
И под моим высотным домом
проходит темная вода.

Глубинная струя влеченья.
Печали светлая струя.
Высокая стена прощенья.
И боли четкая стрела.

"You Scythian," I shall add, "you shrew . . ."
And you'll say, "To hell with you. . . ."

* * *

Release, O rawhide bowstring,
The stillest arrow, a dart
So incredibly hushed, one might suppose
An angel was departing.

In public, we're barely friends,
But for years it's been going on:
Beneath my high-rise window
Dark waters run.

A deep stream of love.
A bright rapids of sorrow.
A high wall of forgiveness.
And pain's clean, piercing arrow.

(translated by Richard Wilbur)

1968

* * *

Не возвращайтесь к былым возлюбленным,
былых возлюбленных на свете пет.
Есть дубликаты —

                 как домик убраный,
где они жили немного лет.

Вас лаем встретит собачка белая,
и расположенные на холме
две рощи — правая, а позже левая —
повторят лай про себя, во мгле.

Два эха в рощах живут раздельные,
как будто в стерео-колонках двух,
все, что ты сделала и что я сделаю,
они разносят по свету вслух.

А в доме эхо уронит чашку,
ложное эхо предложит чай,
ложное эхо оставит на ночь,
когда ей надо бы закричать:

«Не возвращайся ко мне, возлюбленный,
былых возлюбленных на свете нет,
две изумительные изюминки,
хоть и расправятся тебе в ответ...»

А завтра вечером, на поезд следуя,
вы в речку выбросите ключи,
и роща правая, и роща левая
вам вашим голосом прокричит:

«Не покидайте своих возлюбленных.
Былых возлюбленных на свете нет...»

Но вы не выслушаете совет.

1974

36

DO NOT RETURN TO YOUR OLD LOVES

Do not return to your old loves,
there are no former lovers in the world.
Just duplicates—
                        like the house set in order
where they lived for a few years.

You'll be met by a white dog barking
and two groves of trees on a hill,
one to the right, another to the left,
barking back at each other in the dark.

In each grove a separate echo,
as if they were two stereo speakers
conveying to the world aloud
all you have done and all I shall do.

While inside a false echo
will drop a cup, offer you tea,
keep you for the night,
when it ought to be crying out:

"Do not ever return to me, lover,
there are no former lovers, it is true.
But a tiny raisin on each breast
will swell at the very thought of you."

Then the next evening, watching the train depart,
you'll throw the keys in the stream,
and the trees on the right and the trees on the left
will cry out in your own voice:

"Do not leave your beloved.
There are no former lovers."

But you won't listen.

1974   (translated by Vera Dunham and H. W. Tjalsma)

СТАРАЯ ПЕСНЯ

«По деревне янычары детей отбирают...»
Болгарская народная песня

Пой, Георгий, прошлое болит.
На иконах — конская моча.
В янычары отняли мальца.
Он вернется — родину спалит.

Мы с тобой, Георгий, держим стол.
А в глазах — столетия горят.
Братия насилуют сестер,
И никто не знает, кто чей брат.

И никто не знает, кто чей сын,
материнский вырезав живот.
Под какой из вражеских личин
раненая родина зовет?

Если ты, положим, янычар,
не свои ль сжигаешь алтари,
где чужие — можешь различать,
но не понимаешь, где свои.

Безобразя рощи и ручьи,
человеком сделавши на миг,
кто меня, Георгий, отлучил
от древесных родичей моих?

Вырванные груди волоча,
остолбеневая от любви,
мама, отшатнись от палача.

Мама! У него глаза — твои.

1968

OLD SONG

The janissaries carry off our children from village after village.

The past hurts, George, but sing and be merry,
with horses' urine our icons burn.
Each stolen baby becomes a janissary
who will scourge his homeland on his return.

You and I, George, let us drink together,
in our eyes the wild fires of centuries glow.
Each sister is raped by her own brother,
and nobody knows whose brother is who.

With the mother's uterus cut out,
whose son is whose no need to ask.
Our wounded motherland cries out
beneath God knows what enemy mask.

Let us say that we are Turkish soldiers;
aren't we burning our own altars then?
We can understand who our enemies are,
but fail to recognize our own men.

Now ruining forest, field, and stream,
who cut me off, George, tell me please,
the moment I became a human being
from my oldest ancestors, the trees?

Your slashed breast dragging the earth, mother,
transfixed with love more than surprise,
reel back now from your murderer, mother!

Mother, look—he has your eyes!

(translated by William Jay Smith and Vera Dunham)

1968

ТОСКА

Загляжусь ли на поезд с осенних откосов,
забреду ли в вечернюю деревушку —
будто душу высасывают насосом,
будто тянет вытяжка или вьюшка,
будто что-то случилось или случится —
ниже горла высасывает ключицы.

Или поет какая вина запущенная?
Или женщину мучил — и вот наказанье?
Сложишь песню — отпустит,
                                        а дальше — пуще.
Показали дорогу, да путь заказали.

Точно тайный горб на груди таскаю —
тоска такая!

Я забыл, какие у тебя волосы,
я забыл, какое твое дыханье,
подари мне прощенье,
                                        коли виновен,
а простивши — опять одари виною...

1967

ANGUISH

Whether in autumn I stare at a train from a bank
or wander at evening into a village—
it's like a pump sucking out my soul,
like the pull of a damper in a flue—
as if something had happened or were about to happen—
sucking out the collarbone under my throat.

Or is it some neglected guilt complaining?
Did I torment a woman—and am punished thus?
I write a poem—and my anguish subsides—then is
                    worse than before.
The road is opened, and cut off once more.
It's like dragging a secret hump in one's chest,
this anguish.

I can't remember the color of your hair,
I can't remember how your breath felt;
Forgive me then—
                    if I am guilty,
and when I'm forgiven once again give me guilt.

(translated by William Jay Smith and Nicholas Fersen)

1967

СМЕРТЬ ШУКШИНА

Хоронила Москва Шукшина,
хоронила художника, то есть
хоронила страна мужика
и активную совесть.

Он лежал под цветами на треть,
недоступный отныне.
Он свою удивленную смерть
предсказал всенародно в картине.

В каждом городе он лежал
на отвесных российских простынках.
Называлось не кинозал —
просто каждый пришел и простился.

Он сегодняшним дням — как двойник.
Когда зябко курил он чинарик,
так же зябла, подняв воротник,
вся страна в поездах и на нарах.

Он хозяйственно понимал
край как дом — где березы и хвойники.
Занавесить бы черным Байкал,
словно зеркало в доме покойника.

ON THE DEATH OF SHUKSHIN

Moscow was burying Shukshin,
burying an artist;
the nation was burying a man,
burying its conscience.

Inaccessible henceforth,
he lay with flowers half covering him,
having publicly foretold his death
by acting it out in a popular film.

Vertically on the screen as on a sheet
he lay in every city: people came by
in what were no longer theaters
simply to stop and say good-by.

He was a double for his time:
When he shivered, puffing on a cigarette butt,
in trains and on wooden bunks the country
turned up its collar, and shivered with him.

He was master of the house
in a country of fir-trees and birches.
Let Lake Baikal be covered with black
as a mirror is draped in mourning.

(translated by William Jay Smith and Vera Dunham)

ВОЛЬНООТПУЩЕННИК ВРЕМЕНИ

Вольноотнущенник Времени возмущает его рабов.
Лауреат Госпремии тех, довоенных годов
ввел формулу Тяжести Времени. Мир к этому не готов.

Его оппонент в полемике выпрыгнул из своих зубов.
Вольноотпущенник Времени восхищает его рабов.

Был день моего рождения. Чувствовалась духота.
Ночные персты сирени, протягиваясь с куста,
губкою в винном уксусе освежали наши уста.

Отец мой небесный, Время, испытывал на любовь.
Созвездье Быка горело. С низин подымался рев —
в деревне в хлеву от ящура живьем сжигали коров.

Отец мой небесный, Время, безумен Твой часослов!
На неподъемных веках стояли гири часов.
Пьяное эхо из темени кричало, ища коробок,
что Мария опять беременна, а мир опять не готов...

Вольноотпущенник Времени вербует ему рабов.

SERVING TIME

Time's freedman rouses the anger of Time's slaves:
A physicist laureled and locked up in those pre-war days
worked out a formula for the weight of Time. The world wasn't
ready for it.

His antagonist in the debate threw a regular fit:
Time's freedman clearly entrances Time's slaves.

It was my birthday—hot and muggy, hard to breathe;
but at night the lilac branches reached out to me
refreshing evangelical lilac sponges soaked in vinegar.

Time, our heavenly father, was testing us all for love:
Taurus shone in the heavens, but you could hear a roar from the
valleys:
the cows with hoof-and-mouth disease had to be burned alive.

Time, our heavenly father, your book of hours is insane!
On eyelids eternally closed rests the weight of hours.
A man in the dark, drunkenly seeking his matchbox,
cries: "Mary is pregnant again, and again the world is not
ready! . . ."

Time's freedman recruits more slaves for Time.

(translated by William Jay Smith and Vera Dunham)

ИРОНИЧЕСКАЯ ЭЛЕГИЯ, РОДИВШАЯСЯ В ВЕСЬМА СКОРБНЫЕ МИНУТЫ, КОГДА НЕ ПИШЕТСЯ

Я — в кризисе. Душа нема.
«Ни дня без строчки», — друг мой точит.
А у меня —
ни дней, ни строчек.

Поля мои лежат в глуши.
Погашены мои заводы.
И безработица души
зияет страшною зевотой.

И мой критический истец
в статье напишет, что, окрысясь,
в бескризиснейшей из систем
один переживаю кризис.

Мой друг, мой северный, мой неподкупный друг,
хорош костюм, да не по росту.

Внутри все ясно и вокруг —
но не поется.

Я деградирую в любви.
Дружу с оторвою трактирною.
Не деградируете вы —
я деградирую.

Был крепок стих, как рафинад.
Свистал хоккейным бомбардиром.
Я разучился рифмовать.
Не получается.

AN IRONICAL ELEGY BORN IN THOSE MOST DISTRESSING MOMENTS WHEN . . . ONE CANNOT WRITE

I'm in a crisis. My spirit is mute.
"A line a day," my friend insists.
But I have neither
Days nor lines.

My fields lie fallow;
My factories are dark.
My soul, unemployed,
Gapes, yawning wide.

My critic, my accuser,
Will say with a snarl
That in this most immune-to-crisis system
I alone experience a crisis.

My incorruptible fellow countryman,
The suit is perfect, but it doesn't fit.
Everything's clear inside and out—
But poetry doesn't come . . .

I go to pieces in love,
Take to squiring a cheap whore.
You don't go to pieces—
I do.

My verse was solid—like crystal;
A hockey puck, it zinged to its goal.
But I can't rhyme any more;
I've lost the knack.

Чужая птица издали
простонет перелетным горем.
Умеют хором журавли.
Но лебедь не умеет хором.

О чем, мой серый, на ветру
ты плачешь белому Владимиру?
Я этих нот не подберу.
Я деградирую.

Семь поэтических томов
в стране выходит ежесуточно.
А я друзей и городов
бегу как бешеная сука.

в похолодавшие леса
и онемевшие рассветы,
где деградирует весна
на тайном переломе к лету...

Но верю я — моя родня,
две тысячи семьсот семнадцать
поэтов нашей Федерации
стихи напишут за меня.

Они не знают деградации.

A migratory bird
Will mourn in flight.
Cranes sing in unison;
A swan will not.

Gray bird, what do you lament
In the wind before white Vladimir?
I cannot catch those notes;
I go to pieces.

Seven books of poetry
Are published daily;
But I flee friends and towns,
A mad dog,

Into forests gone to frost,
Into dawns turned numb,
Where spring goes to pieces,
Breaking secretly into summer.

And yet I trust my colleagues—
The twenty-five hundred and fifteen
Poets of our federation;
They will write poems even if I can't;

They never go to pieces.

(translated by William Jay Smith and Nicholas Fersen)

Четырнадцать тысяч пиитов
страдают во мгле Лужников.
Я выйду в эстрадных софитах —
последний читатель стихов.

Разинувши рот, как минеры,
скажу в ликование:
«Желаю прослушать Смурновых
неопубликованное!»

Три тыщи великих Смурновых
захлопают, как орлы

с трех тыщ этикеток «Минводы»,
пытаясь взлететь со скалы,
ревя, как при взлете в Орли.

И хор, содрогнув батисферы,
сольется в трехтысячный стих.
Мне грянут аплодисменты
за то, что я выслушал их.

Толпа поэтессок минорно
автографов ждет у кулис.
Доходит до самоубийств!
Скандирующие сурово
Смурновы, Смурновы, Смурновы,
желают на «бис».

И снова как реквием служат,
я выйду в прожекторах,
родившийся, чтобы слушать
среди прирожденных орать.

MONOLOGUE OF THE WORLD'S LAST
POETRY READER
(POETRY DAY, 1999)

In the dark, in the huge sports arena,
fourteen thousand great bards are packed tight.
Now I, the last poetry reader,
will step into the glare of the lights.

Mouth agape, like a soldier who's probing
a mine field, I'll grandly declare:
"The Smurnov Brothers' unpublished poems
are what *I* want to hear."

And three thousand Smurnovs, of great stature,
clap and flap like the eagles on three
thousand bottles of "Mineral Water"
trying to fly from a cliff, with a scream
as when jet planes take off from Orly.

Now their three-thousand-voiced declamation
of their verse shakes their own bathyspheres.
I'm given a thunderous ovation
because I have lent them my ears.

Lady poets, despondently waiting
for autographs, throng the stage door.
(Several suicides litter the floor!)
"The Smurnovs! The Smurnovs!" In strict cadence,
they count out the measure,
and demand an encore.

Once again, a priest serving a Missa
for the souls of the dead, I'll come out:
I, who was born just to listen
to those who were born just to shout.

51

Заслуги мои небольшие,
сутул и невнятен мой век,
средь тысячей небожителей —
единственный человек.

Меня пожалеют и вспомнят.
Не то, что бывал я пророк,
а что не берег перепонки,
как раньше гортань не берег.

«Скажи в меня, женщина, горе,
скажи в меня счастье!
Как плачем мы, выбежав в поле,
но чаще, но чаще

нам попросту хочется высвободить
невысказанное, заветное...
Нужна хоть кому-нибудь исповедь,
как Богу, которого нету!»

Я буду любезен народу
не тем, что творил монумент, —
невысказанную ноту
понять и услышать сумел.

My merits are slight, and I live in
a murky, malformed century;
among thousands who dwell in the heavens,
there's but one human—me.

I'll be pitied but also remembered:
not as prophet but simply because
I did not spare my tympanic membranes—
as I hadn't, when young, spared my voice.

"Let me hear all about your woes, woman;
and your happiness: How,
when we've dashed out into the wide open,
we weep. Yet more and more, now,

"all we want is to cast off our burden—
to release close-held things left unsaid . . .
People *have* to confess to *some*body,
as to God, Who's conveniently dead."

So I shall be dear to the people,
not for rearing my own monument,
but simply because I was able
to grasp what unspoken words meant.

(translated by Guy Daniels)

ВОЙНА

С иными мирами связывая,
глядят глазами отцов
дети —
        широкоглазые
перископы мертвецов.

WAR

With the open eyes of their dead fathers
Toward other worlds they gaze ahead—
Children who, wide-eyed, become
Periscopes of the buried dead.

(translated by William Jay Smith and Vera Dunham)

МОЛИТВА

Боже, ведь я же Твой стебель,
что ж меня отдал толпе?
Боже, что я Тебе сделал?
Что я не сделал Тебе?

PRAYER

Lord, I grow for Thee, for Thee alone,
I am Thy stalk; why then abandon me
To this mob? What is it, Lord, that I have done?
What have I ever not done, Lord, for Thee?

(translated by William Jay Smith and Vera Dunham)

* * *

— Мама, кто там вверху, голенастенький —
руки в стороны — и парит?
— Знать, инструктор лечебной гимнастики.
Мир не может за ним повторить.

PICTURE GALLERY

"Mama, who's that funny man up there
  Flying with his arms out off that cross?"
"That must be some instructor of calisthenics, dear,
  Whose act may be tough to follow, of course."

(translated by William Jay Smith and Vera Dunham)

МОРОЗНЫЙ ИППОДРОМ

В. Аксенову

Табуном рванулись трибуны к стартам.
В центре — лошади,

        вкопанные в наст.
Ты думаешь, Вася,

            мы на них ставим?
Они, кобылы, поставили на нас.

На меня поставила вороная иноходь
Яблоки по крупу — е-мое...
Умеет крупно конюшню вынюхать.
Беру все финиши, а выигрыш — ее.

Королю кажется, что он правит.
Людям кажется, что им — они.
Природа и рощи на нас поставили.
А мы — гони!

Колдуют лошади, они шепочут.
К столбу Ханурик примерз цепочкой.
Все-таки 43°...
Птица замерзла в воздухе, как елочная игрушка.
Мрак, надвигаясь с востока, земерз посредине

                неба, как шторка
у испорченного фотоаппарата.
А у нас в Переделкине, в Доме творчества, были

                окрыты 16 форточек.
Около каждой стоял круглый плотный комок

                комнатного воздуха
Он состоял из сонного дыхания, перегара,

                тяжелых идей.
Некоторые закнопливают фортки марлей,
чтобы идеи не вылетали из комнаты,
как мухи.

WINTER AT THE TRACK

To Vasili Aksyonov

The stands go stampeding to the starting post
Down to where the horses paw the ground.
And, Vasya, you think we're betting on them?
They're betting on us—it's the other way round.

That black mare has put all her money on me—
Just look at her dappled rump;
A hot tip tells her whom to pick;
And I always win, but the take is hers.

So the rulers think it is they who rule,
While the people think they rule the rulers.
The woods and the hills have gambled on us;
So what can we do but race like hell?

The horses whisper, chafing at the bit.
Barfly pisses on the post, linked to it
By a frozen yellow chain:
                     it is forty below.
A Christmas tree ornament, a bird freezes up there.
Night, moving in from the east, is caught congealed mid-air,
The shutter of a broken camera.
But at Peredelkino, in the writers' club,
Sixteen windows are open a crack.
In front of each hangs a chunk of frozen air—
Congealed hot air.
Some writers cover the windows with gauze
So their portentous ideas won't escape like flies.
And the air balloons, sagging, thick and slimy,
As with curds in a cloth.

Horses gaze about them, penned up in cities
Like groves of dappled four-trunked trees.

У тех воздух свисал тугой и плотный,
как творог в тряпочке...

Взирают лошади в городах:
как рощи в яблоках о четырех стволах...

Свистят Ханурику.
                    Но кто свистит?
Свисток считает, что он свистит.
Сержант считает, что он свистит.
Закон считает, что он свистит.

Планета кружится в свистке горошиной,
но в чьей свистульке? Кто свищет? Глядь —
упал Ханурик. Хохочут лошади —
кобыла Дунька, Судьба, конь Блед.

Хохочут лошади.
Их стоны жутки:
«Давай, очкарик! Нажми! Бодрей!»
Их головы покачиваются,
                    как на парашютиках,
на паре, выброшенном из ноздрей.
                    Понятно, мгновенно замерзшем.
Все-таки 45°...
У ворот ипподрома лежал Ханурик.
Он лежал навзничь. Слева — еще пять.
Над его круглым ртом,
короткая, как вертикальный штопор,
открытый из перочинного ножа, стояла
замерзшая Душа.
Она была похожа на поставленную торчком
винтообразную сосульку.
Видно, испарялась по спирали,
да так и замерзла.
И как, бывает, в сосульку вмерзает листик или веточка,
внури ее вмерзло доказательство добрых дел,

Now they're whistling at Barfly,
But who is whistling?
The whistle thinks the whistle's whistling.
The policeman thinks that he is whistling.
The law thinks that it is whistling.

The planet twirls, a pea in a whistle,
But in whose whistle? Who's whistling—wait!
Look, Barfly's down. And the others laugh—
Russian Filly, Pale Horse, Fate.

The horses laugh,
Making terrible sounds:
"Come on, Egghead, let's go! Get a move on!"
While their heads sway on tiny parachutes
Of steam exhaled from their nostrils
And frozen at once.

It is forty-five below:
Barfly lies at the starting post—
On his back: to the left, five others.
Above his open mouth, blunt as a corkscrew
Sticking up from a penknife, his frozen soul,
A screw-shaped icicle protruding into the air;
It has spiraled and condensed.
And as a leaf or twig freezes in an icicle,
Frozen within is its final Certificate of Good Deeds;
(In reality, the denunciation of a neighbor for not turning off
                                                    his radio).

Souls like empty bottles are poised above the other horses,
While among their bodies wanders an angel.
In a street-cleaner's smock, it strolls along,
Collecting the souls, the empty bottles,
Drawing its finger carefully over each to see if it is broken,
Sadly tossing the rejects over its shoulder,
Leaving behind the print of horseshoes in the snow . . .

взятое с собой. Это был обрывок заявления
на соседа за невыключенный радиоприемник.
Над соседними тоже стояли Души, как пустые бутылки.
Между тел бродил Ангел.
Он был одет в сатиновый халат подметальщика.
Он собирал Души, как порожние бутылки.
                                        Внимательно
проводил пальцем — нет ли зазубрин.
Бракованные скорбно откидывал через плечо.
Когда он отходил, на снегу оставались отпечатки
                        следов с подковками...

...А лошадь Ангел — в дыму морозном
ноги растворились,

                        как в азотной кислоте,
шейку шаловливо отогнула, как полозья,
сама, как саночки, скользит на животе!..

1967

And the Angel-Horse, in the frozen haze,
Legs dissolving as in nitric acid,
Playfully arches its neck like the curved runner of a sleigh,
And then, on its belly, slides away.

(translated by Willam Jay Smith and Max Hayward)

1967

НЕ ЗАБУДЬ

Человек надел трусы,
майку синей полосы,
джинсы белые, как снег,
надевает человек.
Человек надел пиджак,
на него нагрудный знак
под названьем «ГТО».
Сверху он надел пальто.

На него, стряхнувши пыль,
он надел автомобиль.
Сверху он надел гараж
(тесноватый — но как раз!),
Сверху он надел жену,
и вдобавок не одну,
сверху он надел наш двор,
как ремень надел забор,
сверху наш микрорайон,
область надевает он.
Опоясался как рыцарь
государственной границей.
И, качая головой,
надевает шар земной.
Черный космос натянул,
крепко звезды застегнул,
Млечный Путь — через плечо,
сверху — кое-что еще...

Человек глядит вокруг.
Вдруг —
у созвездия Весы
он вспомнил, что забыл часы.

DO NOT FORGET

Somewhere a man puts on his shorts,
his blue-striped T-shirt,
his blue jeans;
a man puts on
his jacket on which there is a button
reading COUNTRY FIRST,
and over the jacket, his topcoat.

Over the topcoat,
after dusting it off, he puts on his automobile,
and over that he puts on his garage
(just big enough for his car),
over that his apartment courtyard,
and then he belts himself with the courtyard wall.
Then he puts on his wife
and after her the next one
and then the next one;
and over that he puts on his subdivision
and over that his county
and like a knight he then buckles on
the borders of his country;
and with his head swaying,
puts on the whole globe.

Then he dons the black cosmos
and buttons himself up with the stars.
He slings the Milky Way over one shoulder,
and after that some secret beyond.

He looks around:
Suddenly
in the vicinity of the constellation Libra
he recalls that he has forgotten his watch.

(Где-то тикают они
позабытые, одни?..)

Человек снимает страны,
и моря, и океаны,
и машину, и пальто.
Он без Времени — ничто.

Он стоит в одних трусах,
держит часики в руках.
На балконе он стоит
и прохожим говорит:
«По утрам, надев трусы,
НЕ ЗАБУДЬТЕ ПРО ЧАСЫ!»

Somewhere it must be ticking
(all by itself).
The man takes off the countries,
the sea,
the oceans,
the automobile, and the topcoat.
He is nothing without Time.

Naked he stands on his balcony
and shouts to the passers-by:
"For God's sake, do not forget your watch!"

(translated by William Jay Smith and Vera Dunham)

ОБЩИЙ ПЛЯЖ № 2

По министрам, по актерам,
желтой пяткою своей
солнце жарит
                   полотером
по паркету из людей!

Пляж, пляж —
хоть стоймя, но все же ляжь.

Ноги, прелести творенья,
этажами — как поленья.
Уплотненность, как в аду.
Мир в трехтысячном году.

Карты, руки, клочья кожи,
как же я тебя найду?
В середине зонт, похожий
на подводную звезду, —
8 спин, ног 8 пар.
Упоительный поп-арт!

Пляж, пляж,
где работают лежа,
                   а филонят стоя,
где маскируются, раздеваясь,
где за 10 коп. ты можешь увидеть будущее —
«От горизонта одного — к горизонту многих...»
«Извиняюсь, вы не видели мою ногу?
Размер 37... Обменили...»

«Как же, вот сейчас видала —
в облачках она витала.
Пара крылышков на ей,
как подвязочки!
Только уточняю: номер 38½...».

PUBLIC BEACH NO. 2

Striking actors and ministers alike
with its yellow buffer-heel,
the sun, a polisher,
                    rubs
a parquet made of people.

Even though it's more like standing side by side,
beach, beach, now lie still.

Legs, wonders of creation,
stacked like cordwood—
to the saturation point, as in hell—
the world in the year three thousand.

Cards and hands and shreds of skin,
how will I ever find you?
An umbrella in the center
like a starfish in the sea—
8 backs, 8 pairs of legs—
most beguiling Pop art!

Beach, beach,
where you work lying down
                        and neck standing up,
where undressing is a disguise,
where for 10 kopecks you can read your future—
"From one man's view—to the view of many . . ."
"Excuse me, have you seen my foot?
Size 9 . . . Got swapped . . ."

Yes, of course, just now I saw it
off there floating among the clouds,
a pair of wings attached
like garters!
Only let's get the size right—10½. . . ."

71

Горизонты растворялись
между небом и водой,
облаками, островами,
между камнем и рукой.

На матрасе — пять подружек,
лицами одна к одной,
как пять пальцев в босоножке
перетянуты тесьмой.

Пляж и полдень — продолженье
той божественной ступни.
Пошевеливает Время.
Пошевелятся они.

Я люблю уйти в сиянье,
где границы никакой.
Море — полусостоянье
между небом и землей,

между водами и сушей,
между многими и мной;
между вымыслом и сущим,
между телом и душой.

Как в насыщенном растворе,
что-то вот произойдет:
суша, растворяясь в море,
переходит в небосвод.

И уже из небосвода
что-то возвращалось к нам
вроде Бога и природы
и хожденья по водам.

Horizons dissolved
between water and sky,
clouds and islands,
rock and hand.

Five girl friends stretched out on one mattress,
lying cheek to cheek
like five toes on a bare foot
tied with ribbon.

High noon on the beach—an extension
of that heavenly bare foot.
Time gives signs of stirring;
they will stir along with time.

I love to escape
into boundless effulgence,
into the sea partaking
of both heaven and earth,

both water and land,
both the many and me;
both fantasy and truth,
both body and soul.

Something is about to happen
as in a saturated solution:
land, dissolving in the sea,
changes into heaven's arch.

And from heaven's arch
already something has returned to us,
something akin to God and nature
and to walking on the waters.

Понятно, Бог был невидим.
Только треугольная чайка
                  замерла в центре неба,
белая и тяжело дышащая, —
                  как белые плавки Бога...

But, of course, God is invisible.
Only the triangle of a gull
                    hung motionless at heaven's center,
white, breathing heavily, —
                    like God's white fins. . . .

(translated by William Jay Smith and Nicholas Fersen)

ХОР НИМФ

Я 41-я на Плисецкую,
26-я на пледы чешские,
30-я на Таганку,
35-я на Ваганьково,
кто на Мадонну — запись на Морвокзале,
а Вы с ребенком, тут не стояли!
Кто был девятая, станет десятой,
Борисова станет Мусатовой,
я 16-я к глазному,
75-я на Глазунова,
110-я на аборты
(придет очередь — подработаю),
26-я на фестивали,
а Вы с ребенком, тут не стояли!
47-я на автодетали,
(меня родили — и записали),
я уже 1000-я на автомобили
(меня записали — потом родили),
что дают? кому давать?
а еще мать!
Я 45-я за «35-ми»,
а Вы с ребенком, чего тут пялитесь?
Кто на Мадонну — отметка в 10-ть.
А Вы с ребенком — и не надейтесь!
Не вы, а я — 1-я на среду,
а Вы — первая куда следует...

Отстоявши полночные смены,
не попавши в священный реестр,
вы, читательница поэмы,
может, вы героиня и есть?

A CHORUS OF NYMPHS

I'm 41st in line for Plisetskaya,
26th for plaid blankets from Czechoslovakia,
30th for a ticket to the Taganka,
35th for a place in Vagankovo Cemetery,
whoever wants to see the Madonna—sign up
at Seaport Hall—hey, you with the kid,
you weren't in line before!
Whoever was ninth goes back to tenth,
Rimskaya becomes Korsakova,
I'm 16th at the optician's,
and 75th for Glazunov,
110th for an abortion
(not pregnant now, but ready·when my turn comes).
You with the kid, you weren't here before,
47th for spare car parts
(they signed me up at birth).
No. 1000 for a new car
(signed up before birth).
What are they giving out? Who should be bribed?
And you're a mother besides!
I'm 45th behind everybody with a 35,
and, you with the kid, what are you staring at?
Those who want to see the Madonna, check in at ten o'clock.
But, you with the kid, you won't make it.
Because I'm first for Wednesday,
and you're first to go to hell.

Working the night shift,
not one of the elect,
are you, dear reader, perhaps
the heroine of this poem?

Просветлев от забот ежегодных,
отстояла очередя.
И в Москву прилетела Джоконда,
чтоб секунду взглянуть на Тебя.

Illuminated by perennial cares,
you've waited in line.
And the Gioconda has flown to Moscow
to gaze for an instant on Thee.

(translated by Vera Dunham and H. W. Tjalsma)

ПИР

Человек явился в лес,
всем принес деликатес:

лягушонку
дал сгущенку,

дал ежу,
что — не скажу,

а единственному волку
дал охотничью водку,

налил окуню в пруды
мандариновой воды.

Звери вежливо ответили:
«Мы еды твоей отведали.
Чтоб такое есть и пить,
надо человеком быть.
Что ж мы попусту сидим,
хочешь, мы тебя съедим?»

Человек сказал в ответ:
«Нет.
Мне ужасно неудобно,
но я очень несъедобный.
Я пропитан алкоголем,
алохолом, аспирином.
Вы меня видали голым?
Я от язвы оперируем.

Я глотаю утром водку,
следом тассовскую сводку,
две тарелки, две газеты,
две магнитные кассеты,
и коллегу по работе,

THE FEAST

A man appeared in the wood,
bringing everyone something good.

A sweet jelly roll
for the tadpole;

I won't reveal
the hedgehog's meal.

For the one wolf
he brought Smirnoff;
for the perch in the stream
a tangerine.

The beasts said:
"We don't mean to be finicky,
but we haven't seen anything
a creature could eat or drink.
In order to consume any of this stuff
you'd have to be a man. So
take back your ragout,
we think we'll eat you!"

The man said:
"Whoa,
it's not that I think you're suggestible,
but I must tell you that I'm indigestible.
I reek of alcohol, Ex-lax, and aspirin.
I'm a wreck—to be crude,
have you seen me in the nude?

"In the morning I down a demitasse
of vodka, the news from TASS,
two plates, two papers, two cassettes,
a colleague from work, two apples for dessert
dipped in DDT.

и два яблока в компоте,
опыленных ДДТ,
и т. д.

Плюс сидит в печенках враг,
курит импортный табак.
В час четыре сигареты.
Это
убивает в день
сорок тысяч лошадей.

Вы хотите никотин?»
Все сказали: «Не хотим,
жаль тебя. Ты — вредный, скушный:
если хочешь — ты нас скушай».

Человек не рассердился
и, подумав, согласился.

And then somebody
sits in my liver chain-smoking Gauloises.
Enough cigarettes to kill
forty thousand horses a day.
You want all that nicotine, what do you say?"

"We say NAY.
We are sorry, to be sure—you're pitiful,
and, what's more,
an inedible bore.
We'd rather be dead.
You want to? Eat us instead."

The man took heed,
thought—
            and agreed.

(translated by Vera Dunham and H. W. Tjalsma)

Н Т Р

«Моя бабушка — староверка,
но она —
научно-техническая революционерка.
Кормит гормонами кабана.

Научно-технические коровы
следят за Харламовым и Петровым,
и, прикрываясь ночным покровом,
сексуал-революционерка Сударкина,
в сердце
                 как в трусики-безразмерки,
умещающая пол-Краснодара,
подрывает основы
семьи,
             частной собственности
                                    и государства.

Научно-технические обмены
отменны.
Посылаем Терисихору —
получаем «Пепсиколу».

«И все-таки это есть Революция —
в умах, в быту и в народах целых.
К двенадцати стрелки часов крадутся —
но мы носим лазерные, без стрелок!

Я — попутчик
                 научно-технической революции.
При всем уважении к коромыслам
хочу, чтобы в самой дыре завалющей
был водопровод
                 и свобода мысли.

TECHNOLOGY

My grandmother is an Old Believer,
a technological revolutionary;
she fattens her pig on hormones.

Her technological cows
watch a hockey game on TV.
And under cover of night,
taking half her provincial city
to heart,
        into her elastic panties,
there is a sexual revolutionary
who undermines the basis
of the family,
        private property,
                and the state.

Official technological exchanges
are a good idea:
We send them our best ballerinas
and get Pepsi-Cola in return.

And yet this is a Revolution—
in the minds and lives of peoples.
Toward midnight the hands of clocks get stolen,
but we wear digital watches
        that have no hands.

I'm a fellow traveler
        of this technological revolution.
With all due respect to samovars,
in the very middle of this provincial hole,
I long for plumbing and freedom
        of thought.

Революция в опасности.
Нужны меры.
Она саботажникам не по нутру.
Научно — технические контрреволюционеры
Не едят синтетическую икру.

1973

But this Revolution is in danger!
S.O.S.
Technological counterrevolutionaries,
refuse to eat synthetic caviar!

(translated by William Jay Smith and Vera Dunham)

1973

ЧЕРНОЕ ЕРНИЧЕСТВО

Когда спекулянты рыночные
прицениваются к Чюрлёнису,
поэты уходят в рыцари
черного ерничества.

Их самоубийственный вывод:
стать ядом во имя истины.
Пусть мир в отвращении вырвет,
а следовательно— очистится,

Но самое черное ерничество,
заботясь о человеке,
химической червоточиной
покрыло души и реки.

Но самые черные ерники
в белых воротничках,
не веря ни в Бога, ни в черта,
кричат о святых вещах.

Верю в черную истину,
верю в белую истину,
верю в истину синюю —
не верю в истину циника...

Мой бедный, бедный ерник!
Какие ж твои молитвы?
У лица дождевые дворники
машут опасной бритвой.

Тоска твою душу ест,
вот ты хохмишь у фрески,
где тащит страдалец крест:
«Христос на воскреснике».

BLACK BUFFOONERY

When black marketeers discuss what is
the going price of a Chiurlionis,
poets assume the right to be
knights of black buffoonery.

So in ironic suicide
let truth be poison, they decide:
Let the whole world retch until
it spues forth all its ill.

The blackest of buffoonery
is buffoonery that can
pollute the very soul of man
with vitriolic wormholes

And the blackest blasphemers,
the proper white-collared sort,
faithful to neither God nor Devil,
rail against all holy things.

I believe in basic truth
be it black or white or blue.
I believe in what is true;
I won't accept the cynic's truth.

And so, my blaspheming buffoon,
what are your prayers like taking place
while windshield wipers razor-sharp
cut a path before your face?

Sorrow eats your heart out, true,
before a fresco? So you smirk
at Christ who bears the cross for you
"on special Sunday roadwork."

Но мужество не в коверничестве,
а в том, чтоб сказать без робости:
Да сгинет общее ерничество
во имя Светлого Образа!

Поэты — рыцари чина
Светлого Образа.
Да сгинет первопричина
черного ерничества!

Courage is not buffoonery,
it's to speak out unafraid:
"May blasphemy forever fade
in the name of the Bright Visage.

"May poets become the True Knights,
bearers all of Radiant Truth,
and the root of black buffoonery
perish forever from the earth."

(translated by William Jay Smith and Vera Dunham)

ИСПОВЕДЬ

Ну что тебе надо еще от меня?
Чугунна ограда. Улыбка темна.
Я музыка горя, ты музыка лада,
ты яблоко-ада, да не про меня!

На всех континентах твои имена
прославил. Такие отгрохал лампады!
Ты музыка счастья, я нота разлада.
Ну что тебе надо еще от меня?

Смеялась: «Ты ангел?» — я лгал, как змея.
Сказала: «Будь смел» — не вылазил из спален.
Сказала: «Будь первым» — я стал гениален,
ну что тебе надо еще от меня?

Исчерпана плата до смертного дня.
Последний горит под твоим снегопадом.
Был музыкой чуда, стал музыкой яда,
ну что тебе надо еще от меня?

Но и под лопатой спою, не виня:
«Пусть я удобренье для Божьего сада,
ты — музыка чуда, но больше не надо!
Ты случай досады. Играй без меня».

И вздрогнули складни, как створки окна.
И вышла усталая и без наряда.
Сказала: «Люблю тебя. Больше нет сладу.
Ну что тебе надо еще от меня?»

1971

THE ETERNAL QUESTION

What more on this earth do you want from me?
Iron is the railing protecting your smile.
I am all discord, you are all harmony,
But the apple you offer's not from heaven but hell.

I have carried your name far across the sea,
And the purest of candles have lighted for you.
Your music brings joy, while mine brings decay:
What more on this earth do you want from me?

"You're pure?" you said, and, a serpent, I lied.
"Be brave, be a man!" So I slept with each whore.
"Be first!" you cried, and a genius I was:
What more on this earth do you want? What more?

I paid with my life till I couldn't pay more,
I died, and lay burning beneath your snowfall;
My words were of wonder, and you poisoned them all:
What more on this earth do you want? What more?

When they shoveled the last of the earth on my grave,
I still spoke no ill, and had only one claim:
That to freshen God's garden my bones might serve,
And if Error you are, then play your own game.

The mirrors behind you opened into a door,
And glittering, naked you stood before me.
"I love you," you said. "What more then of me—
What more on this earth do you want? What more?"

(translated by William Jay Smith)

1971

93

Voznesensky with Khrushchev behind him.

Close-up of Khrushchev.

Close-up of Voznesensky.

Voznesensky and Robert Kennedy, 1967.

PART II

РЕКВИЕМ

Возложите на море венки.
Есть такой человечий обычай —
в память воинов, в море погибших,
возлагают на море венки.

Здесь, ныряя, нашли рыбаки
десять тысяч стоящих скелетов,
ни имен, ни причин не поведав,
запрокинувших головы к свету,
они тянутся к нам, глубоки.
Возложите на море венки.

Чуть качаются их позвонки,
кандалами прикованы к кладбищу,
безымянные страшные ландыши.
Возложите на море венки.

На одном, как ведро, сапоги,
на другом — на груди амулетка.
Вдовам их не помогут звонки.
Затопили их вместо расстрела,
души их, покидавшие тело,
по воде оставляли круги.

Возложите на море венки
под свирель, барабан и сирены.
Из жасмина, из роз, из сирени
возложите на море венки.

Возложите на землю венки.
В ней лежат молодые мужчины.
Из сирени, из роз, из жасмина
возложите живые венки.

REQUIEM

Lay wreaths on the sea.
Ancient customs decree
that to honor the graves
of sailors lost to the waves
wreaths be laid on the sea.

Here fishermen, diving, found far under
ten thousand skeletons all upright.
Neither name, rank, nor serial number
did they reveal. Heads tilted to the light,
they aspire toward us from the deep.
Lay wreaths on the sea.

One still wears a boot like a bucket,
another, an amulet.
(What good are consoling telephone calls?)
These men weren't shot; they were drowned instead.
Spiraling up from their bodies, their souls
left ripples that spread.

Lay wreaths on the sea.
Made of jasmine and roses and lilac;
to fife and drum and siren
lay wreaths on the sea.

Lay wreaths on the earth:
beneath it young soldiers lie;
of jasmine and roses and lilac
lay fresh wreaths on the earth.

Weave garlands of earth's fair flowers
for pilots who burned in the air high
above it. (You drank with them in their last hours.)
Lay wreaths on the sky.

Заплетите земные цветы
над землею сгоревшим пилотам.
С ними пили вы перед полетом.
Возложите на небо венки.

Пусть стоят они в небе, видны,
презирая закон притяженья,
говоря поколеньям пришедшим:
«Кто живой — возложите венки».

Возложите на Время венки,
в этом вечном огне мы сгорели.
Из жасмина, из белой сирени
на огонь возложите венки.

Let them hang in the sky, plain to see,
scorning the law of gravitation,
and saying to each new generation:
"Let the living lay wreaths."

Lay wreaths on Time, eternal
fire that consumes us all;
of jasmine and white lilac
lay wreaths on the fire.

(translated by Guy Daniels)

ИЮНЬ-68

Лебеди, лебеди, лебеди...
К северу. К северу. К северу!..
Кеннеди... Кеннеди... Кеннеди...
Срезали...

Может, в чужой политике
не понимаю что-то?
Но понимаю залитые
кровью беспомощной щеки!

Баловень телепублики
в траурных лимузинах...
Пулями, пулями, пулями
бешеные полемизируют!..

Помню, качал рассеянно
целой еще головою,
смахивал на Есенина
падающей копною.

Как у того играла,
льнула луна на брови...
Думали — для рекламы,
а обернулось — кровью.

Незащищенность вызова
лидеров и артистов,
прямо из телевизоров
падающих на выстрел!

Ах, как тоскуют корни,
отнятые от сада,
яблоней на балконе
на этаже тридцатом!..

JUNE '68

Wild swans, wild swans, wild swans,
Northward, northward bound
Kennedy . . . Kennedy . . . the heart
Breaks at the sound.

Of foreign politics
Not much may be understood;
But I do understand
A white cheek bathed with blood.

The idol of TV screens
In his funereal auto rides . . .
With bullets, bullets, bullets
Madmen proselytize.

When absently he shook
That head while yet intact
I thought of Yesenin
With his tumbling forelock:

As on that poet's brow
A sickle moon would brood—
For public effect, they thought,
But it proved to be for blood.

How defenseless the challenger,
Politician or poet,
When he topples to gunshot
Right through the TV set!

Oh, the roots of apple trees
Torn from orchard soil
Mourn high on her balcony
There on the thirtieth floor!

Яблони, яблони, яблони —
к дьяволу!..

Яблони небоскребов —
разве что для надгробьев.

Apple trees, apple trees . . .
Curse those bloody trees!

Let skyscraper-apples grieve,
Good but to guard a grave.

(translated by William Jay Smith and Nicholas Fersen)

СТРОКИ РОБЕРТУ ЛОУЭЛЛУ

Мир
праху твоему,
            прозревший президент!
Я многое пойму,
до ночи просидев.

Кепчоночку сниму
с усталого виска.
Мир, говорю, всему,
чем жизнь ни высока...

Мир храпу твоему,
            Великий Океан.
Мир — пахарю в Клину.
Мир,
сан-францисский храм,
чьи этажи, как вздох,
            озонны и стройны,
вздохнут по мне разок,
            как легкие страны.
Мир
паху твоему,
ночной Нью-Йоркский парк,
дремучий, как инстинкт,
            убийствами пропах,
природно возлежишь
меж каменных ножищ.
Что ты понатворишь?
Мир
пиру твоему,
земная благодать,
мир праву твоему
меня четвертовать.

Мир Солнцу самому,
            что гонит мглу, преображает карты,

LINES TO ROBERT LOWELL

Bless
your grave, Mr. President.
You have become clairvoyant.
I shall see things as they are
while I sit and wait for the night.

I'll bare my head and say
    "Bless everything!"

Bless the sound of your waves,
                great ocean.
Bless you, plowman of Klin.

Bless
    the temple of San Francisco's
high levels. As ethereal
        and deep as a breath
this once they'll sigh for me . . .
        the lungs of the nation.

Bless
    your big prick
at night Central Park
rank and thick as an instinct
      reeking of murder
you lie sprawled on your back
      between huge legs of stone—
what now?
Heaven on earth,
bless
your banquet table
Bless your historical privilege
to hack me in bloody pieces.

Bless the sun itself
that drives the night away, transforms
          the maps.

мир сердцу моему
и миллионам солнечных инфарктов.

История, ты стон
    пророков, распинаемых
        крестами;
они сойдут с крестов,
     взовьют еретиков кострами.

Безумствует распад.
Но — все-таки — виват! —
профессия рождать
древней, чем убивать.

Визжат мальцы рожденные
       у повитух в руках,
как трубки телефонные
в притихшие века.

Мир тебе,
Гуго,
миллеровский пес,
    миляга.
Ты не такса, ты туфля,
мокасин с отставшей подошвой.
который просит каши.
Некто Неизвестный напялил тебя
на левую ногу
и шлепает по паркету.
Иногда Он садится в кресло нога на ногу,
и тогда ты становишься под носом вверх,
и всем кажется, что просишь чего-нибудь
со стола.
Ах, Гуго, Гуго... Я тоже чей-то башмак.
Я ощущаю Нечто, надевшее меня...

Мир Неизвестному,
которого нет,
но есть...

Bless my heart
and millions of hearts that stagger
at a touch of the sun.

You, history, are the moan
            of crucified prophets.
When they come down from the cross
heretics will be burned and lofted skyward.

Bless you, producers of the new
who're running mad—I could weep!
Bless you, palaces, crumbling in the flood
of the "cultural revolution"—in Florence.
Everything's sliding apart.

Yet, "Long live everything!"
For the art of creation
is older than the art of killing.

Howling infants are cradled
                    in the hands of midwives
They're the telephone receivers
                    of ages that shall be silent.

Bless you,
Hugo.
Arthur Miller's dog,
a lovely creature.
You're not a dachshund,
you're a slipper,
a moccasin with a gaping sole,
shabby with use.

A certain Unknown Being puts you
on his left foot
and shuffles across the floor.
Sometimes he sits in an armchair
            and crosses his legs,
then you tilt nose upward
            45 degrees.

111

Мир, парусник благой, —
Америку открыл.
Я русский мой глагол
Америке открыл.

В ристалищных лесах
проголосил впервые,
срываясь на верхах,
трагическую музыку России.

Не горло — сердце рву.
Америка, ты — ритм.
Мир брату моему,
что путь мой повторит.

Поэт собой, как в колокол,
колотит в свод обид.
Хоть больно, но звенит...

Мой милый Роберт Лоуэлл,
мир Вашему письму,
печальному навзрыд.
Я сутки прореву,
и все осточертит,

к чему играть в кулак?
                    (пустой или с начинкой?)
Узнать, каков дурак, —
                    простой или начитанный?
Глядишь в сейчас — оно
давнее, чем давно,
величественно, но
дерьмее, чем дерьмо.

Мир мраку твоему.
На то ты и поэт,
что, получая тьму,
ты излучаешь свет.

and everyone thinks
        that you're begging
        a scrap from the table.
Oh Hugo, Hugo . . . I too am someone's
        shoe, I feel the Unknown
        that is wearing me.
Bless the unknown
that does not exist
yet is!

Bless the good ship that sailed
to discover America.
I am bringing to America
the discovery of the Russian tongue.

In cities, in the maze of parks,
I was the first to sound
the agonizing music of Russia
with a voice that fades in the upper ranges.

It's not my throat . . . my heart is lacerated.
America, you're a rhythm.
Bless every fellow poet
who shall walk in my footsteps!

The poet thrusts his body
like a tolling bell
against the dome of insults.
It hurts. But it resounds.

Dear Robert Lowell, bless
your letter.
It has made me sad.
I'll weep for a whole day, hating
everything and everybody.

Why should we play their game?
Why should we try to guess
which hand it's in? Why ask
        a fool to show his credentials!

Ты хочешь мира всем.
Тебе ж не настает.

Куда в такую темь,
мой бедный самолет?
Спи, милая,
дыши
все дольше и ровней.
Да будет мир души
измученной твоей!

Все меньше городок,
горящий на реке,
как милый ремешок
с часами на руке,
Значит,

   опять ты их забыла снять.
Они светятся и тикают.
Я отстегну их тихо-тихо,

     чтоб не спугнуть дыхания,
     заведу
и положу налево, на ощупь,
где должна быть тумбочка...

You speak of today, but this . . .
game is old.
All round us—piles of shit!
and still, real pearls exist.

Bless the darkness around you.
That's why you're a poet
As the night presses inward
you radiate beams of light.

You bless
but are not blessed.

And you, my plane, where are you flying
in this darkness? Sleep, dear,
breathe more deeply, more evenly.
Peace to your tormented spirit!

On the river
as on the dear straps of your watch
the tiny city dwindles, a twinkling dial.
For you forgot to take it off again.
The watch shines and ticks.
I'll unfasten it gently, gently
        so as not to frighten your sleep away.
I'll wind it,
and put it on the left,
feeling my way in the dark
where the night table must be.

(translated by Louis Simpson and Vera Dunham)

115

САН-ФРАНЦИСКО — КОЛОМЕНСКОЕ

Сан-Франциско — это Коломенское.
Это свет посреди холма.
Высота, как глоток колодезный,
холодна.

Я люблю тебя, Сан-Франциско;
испаряются надо мной
перепончатые фронтисписы,
переполненные высотой.

Вечерами кубы парившие
наполняются голубым.
как просвечивающие курильщики
тянут красный, тревожный дым.

Это вырезанное из неба
и приколотое к мостам
угрызение за измену
моим юношеским мечтам.

Моя юность архитектурная,
прикурю об огни твои,
сжавши губы на высшем уровне,
побледневшие от любви.

Как обувка возле отеля
лимузины столпились в ряд.
будто ангелы улетели,
лишь галоши от них стоят.

SAN FRANCISCO IS KOLOMENSKOYE

San Francisco is Kolomenskoye . . .
a light cupped on a slope.
It's as high as the water
drawn from a well is cold.

I love you, San Francisco.
I can see a dissolving
web, a frontispiece
brimming with height.

At night the foggy cubicles
are colored with gold . . .
inhaling the cancerous red smoke
like invisible smokers.

Cut out of the sky
and nailed to the bridges
is my remorse for failure
to keep my promised dreams.

Architecture, the past . . .
let me light my cigarette from you.
My lips, drained by love,
shall inhale at the highest level.

Down there, by the hotel . . .
black limousines in rows, like shoes,
as if the angels
    had flown in a hurry
leaving their black galoshes . . .

Мы — не ангелы. Черт акцизный
шлепнул визу — и хоть бы хны...
Ты вздохни по мне, Сан-Франциско.
Ты, Коломенское,
                вздохни...

We are not angels.
The devil in the tax department
slaps on a stamp and doesn't give a damn . . .
Want me,
       San Francisco.
Want me, Kolomenskoye.

(translated by Louis Simpson and Vera Dunham)

* * *

Ах, московская американочка...
Обернулся Арбатом Бродвей.
На меня приземляется парочка
из Москвы упорхнувших бровей.

Разве мыслимо было подумать,
что в Нью-Йорке, как некогда встарь,
разметавшись, уснем на подушке,
словно русско-английский словарь.

Мировые границы отринем.
Будут стулья в джинсовом тряпье.
Засыпая, ты скажешь мне: «Дриминг...»
«Дрема, дрема», — отвечу тебе.

FROM A DIARY

Ah, you Muscovite American girl
Who makes Broadway the Arbat I know,
Those lashes that you fix on me
Have fluttered down here from Moscow.

Who in his right mind would have thought
That here in New York we'd lie upon
This pillow one day, opened out
Like a Russian-English lexicon?

Let's fling back the borders of the world
While with denim our jeans drape the armchairs in blue.
As you drift off you'll mutter, "I dream . . . I dream . . ."
"Dryoma, dryoma," I'll answer you.

(translated by William Jay Smith)

СОБАКАЛИПСИС

*Посвящается моим четвероногим слушателям
университета Саймон Фрейзер.*

Верю
всякому зверю.
Тем паче
обожаю концерт собачий.

Я читаю полулегальное
вам, борзая,
                       и вам, лягавая.

Билетерами неопознан,
на концерт мой пришел опоссум.
И приталенная, как у коршуна,
на балконе присела кожанка.

Зал мохнат от марихуаны.
В тыщу глаз, рыжий кобель.
В «Откровенни Иоанна»
Упомянут подобный зверь.

Грозный зверь, по имени Фатум,
И по телу всему — зрачки.
Этот зверь —
                       лафа фабриканту,
выпускающему очки!
Трепещите, мамочки-папочки!
Воет волхв —
Ферлингетти.. Овечья шапочка —
в серой шапочке — красный волк.

Поджигатель, певец, повеса,
он прикурил от повестки в суд.
В судное время нам всем повестки.
И это касается псов и сук.

DOGALYPSE

To the dear four-footed friends at my readings

I trust every animal
but especially I adore
dogs in concert

Here I am, reading half-legally
to you, wolfhounds and hound-dogs

A raccoon snuck in
past the ticket-taker
A leather coat perfectly fitted
like a falcon's hood
squeezed into a seat

I still remember that sinuous skin
dying for the lights to dim,
her jaw-breaking yawn
like an acrobat doing the splits
with the bliss of Blok's "La Belle Dame"
arching her back
A dog put out her paws
like the legs of a chaise-longue.
The hall is mossy with marijuana,
mad dog with a thousand eyes
as in Saint John's
apocalyptic visions.
A thousand eyes—
Big business for contact lens-makers!

Bureaucrats, drop dead!
A poet is howling.
Ferlinghetti, sheepskin hat—
a red wolf, in a grey sheep's skin,
A lamb in wolf's clothing,
he lights his joint with a bench warrant.

123

Суди, лохматое поколенье!
Если не явится бог судить —
тех, кто вешает нас в бакалейнях,
тех, кто иудить пришел и удить.

И стоял я, убийца слова,
и скрипел пиджачишко мой —
кожа, содранная с коровы,
фаршированная душой.

Где-то сестры ее мычали
в электродоильниках бигуди.
Елизаветинские медали
у псов поблескивали на груди.

Вам, уставшие от мицуки,
я выкрикиваю привет
от бродячей безухой суки,
у которой медалей нет.

Но зато чта сука — певчая.
И уж ежели даст концерт —
все Карузо отдали бы печени
за господен ее фальцет!

Понимали без перевода
Лапа Драная и Перо,
потом что стихов природа —
Не грамматика, а нутро.

Понимали без перевода,
и не англо-русский словарь,
а небесное, полевое,
и где в музыке не соврал...

In time of Judgment, a warrant hangs over us all.
And this includes studs and bitches.

Shaggy generation, you've got to judge
if God won't judge
those who hangs us in super-markets
those who make like Judas
and make their haul!
So I stood there, a murderer of the Word,
and my jacket creaked—
a cow's hide stuffed with soul.

Somewhere her sisters mooed
in electric milking-curlers.
Medieval medal dog-tags
shine on dogs' chests.

To you, exuding perfume,
I'm shouting the love
of an earless Moscow mutt
who has no medals.

But still I'm a bitch of a singer
and if I gave a concert
all those Carusos would give their livers
for my Master's Voice

Old Rover, old Fido—
They understood without translation—
for the nature of poetry
is not in the grammar but in the gut.

They understood without translation,
No English-Russian dictionary—
only the language of sky and field
and the places where music
hasn't lied.

Я хочу, чтобы меня поняли.
Ну, а тем, кто к стихам глухи,
разъяснит двухметровый колли,
обнаружиая клыки!

They understood by breathing deeply.
Before the Word was God
moon and dog understood each other.

I want to be understood
And to those who are deaf to poetry,
a six-foot collie will explain it all,
fangs bared!

(translated by Lawrence Ferlinghetti, Maureen Sager, Catherine Leach, and Vera Dunham)

ЯБЛОКИ С БРИТВАМИ

Хэллувин, Хэллувин — ну куда Голливуд?! —
детям бритвы дают, детям бритвы дают!

В Хэллувин, в Хэллувин с маскарадными ритмами
по дорогам гуляет осенний пикник.
Воздух яблоком пахнет,

                            но яблоком с бритвами.
На губах перерезанный бритвою крик.

Хэллувин — это с детством и летом разлука.
Кто он? — сука? насмешник? добряк? херувим?
До чего ты страшна, современная скука!
Хэллувин...

Ты мне шлешь поздравленья, слезами облитые,
хэллувиночка, шуточка, детский овал.
Но любовь — это райское яблоко с бритвами.
Сколько раз я надкусывал, сколько давал...

Благодарствую, боже, твоими молитвами,
жизнь — прекрасный подарочек. Хэллувин.
И за яблоки с бритвами, и за яблоки

                                с бритвами
ты простишь нас. И мы тебя, Боже, простим.

Но когда-нибудь в Судное время захочет
и тебя и меня на Судилище том
допросить усмехающийся ангелочек,
семилетний пацан с окровавленным ртом!

HALLOWEEN APPLES

Halloween, Halloween, beyond Hollywood—
boys and girls given razor blades . . .

Halloween, baby monsters roving the streets, Halloween,
Season of masks and leaves hurrying . . .

Air smells like apples, but apples with razorblades.
There's a cry sliced by a razor blade.

It's Halloween, our glad summer is gone,
Who is that rotten pig, that clown, that slimy St. Nicholas?
The boredom is ghastly, ghastly, ghastly!
Hallowee . . . . .

And your letter arrived full of tears, my Halloween girl,
our love was a prank, wasn't it?
Your child cameo-face,
and our apple of immortality had razor blades in it—
I myself have eaten it, and I have given it too.

I thank God always through my prayers
for life is a magnificent little old gift.
                                    Halloween.

You'll forgive us for these razor blade apples
                        and we'll forgive you too.

But when the graves open at the Last Day
a tiny angel with a curious smile
will call both God and me for cross examination—
a seven year old child with a bloody mouth.

                            (translated by Robert Bly)

ЗАБАСТОВКА СТРИПТИЗА

Стриптиз бастует! Стриптиз бастует!
Над мостовыми канкан лютует.

Грядут бастующие — в тулупах, джинсах.
«Черта в ступе!
                    Не обнажимся!»
Эксплуататоров теснят, отбрехиваясь.
Что там блеснуло?
                    Держи штрейкбрехершу!

Под паранджою чинарь запаливают,
а та на рожу чулок напяливает.

Ку-ку, трудящиеся эстрады!
Вот ветеранка в облезлом страусе,
едва за тридцать — в тираж пора:
«Ура, сестрички,
                    качнем права!
Соцстрахование, процент с оваций
и пенсий ранних — как в авиации...»

«А производственные простуды?»
Стриптиз бастует.
«А факты творческого зажима?
Не обнажимся!»
Полчеловечества вопит рыдания:
«Не обнажимся.
Мы — солидарные!»

Полы зашивши
(«Не обнажимся!»),
в пальто к супругу
жена ложится!

Лежит, стервоза,
и издевается:

STRIPTEASE ON STRIKE

The strippers are out on strike,
a fierce cancan drums on the sidewalks—
the strikers are marching in fur coats and blue jeans:
"To hell with it!
        We won't strip no more!"

They shove their exploiters, kick and claw them.
"Look at that bright bare ass!—
        Stop the scabbing bitch!"
There's one in a yashmak—sneaking a smoke behind it,
and that one's pulled a stocking over her face.

"Hey there, workers of the stage!
See that old-timer with her mangy ostrich feathers?
Just pushing thirty and it's time to retire,
come on, girls, stick up for your rights:
social security, a commission on encores
and early pensions, like in the air force.

"And what about colds caught in line of duty?"
The strippers are out on strike.
"And they're always trampling
on our sensibilities!
We won't strip no more!"

Half of mankind cries out with them:
"Why should we bare ourselves?
Let's show our solidarity!"

A woman gets in her husband's bed
all sewn up tight in a heavy coat:
"We won't strip no more."

She just lies there, the bitch,
and pokes fun at the man:
"Cats don't take their coats off either!"

«Мол, кошки тоже
не раздеваются...»

А оперируемая санитару.
«Сквозь платье режьте — я солидарна!»

«Мы не позируем», —
вопят модели.
«Пойдем позырим,
на Венеру надели
синенький халатик в горошек, с коротенькими
рукавами!..»
Мир юркнул в раковину.
Бабочки, сложив крылышки, бешено
                          заматывались в куколки.
Церковный догматик заклеивал тряпочками
нагие чресла Сикстинской капеллы,
                          штопором он пытался
вытащить пуп из микеланджеловского
Адама
Первому человеку пуп не положен!

Весна бастует. Бастуют завязи.
Спустился четкий железный
                          занавес.
Бастует там истина.
                 Нагая издавна,
она не издана, а если издана,
то в ста обложках под фразой фиговой —
попробуй выковырь!

Земля покрыта асфальтом города.
Мир хочет голого,
                 голого,
                          голого.
У мира дьявольский аппетит.
Стриптиз бастует. Он победит!

A woman under the knife
says to the surgeon:
"Cut through my dress! Solidarity forever!"

"We're sick of posing,"
the models yell,
"Let's go look at Venus de Milo—
they've got her up
in short-sleeved navy polka dots."

The world's ducking into its shell,
butterflies fold their wings
and struggle back, frantic,
into their cocoons.

A zealot's covering up the
naked loins in the Sistine Chapel.
and, with a corkscrew, he's trying
to take the navel out of Michelangelo's Adam:
the First Man wasn't supposed to have one.
Same mentality as the old biddies of Sarato.

Coverers-up of the world unite!
Spring is on strike, so are the buds—
There is the Iron Curtain.

Truth is on strike. Always naked,
it can't be printed, and if it is,
there's a fig leaf on it.
How to get at it?

The earth's under asphalt,
it longs to be naked.
The world has a hell of an appetite.
The world will win.
The stripteasers will win!

(translated by Max Hayward)

БЕРЕГ ЛОНГАЙЛАНДА

Р. Раушенбергу

Здесь отпечатки пальцев птичьи
на утренних песках лежат —
как треугольнички девичьи
от испарившихся наяд.

LONG ISLAND BEACH
To Robert Rauschenberg

I come on the footprints of sea gulls
Here on the shore at dawn
Like the print of their sex that mermaids left
When with the tide they've gone.

(translated by William Jay Smith)

НЬЮ-ЙОРКСКИЕ ЗНАЧКИ

> *Кока-кола. Колокола.*
> *Точно звонница, голова...*
> «Треугольная груша».

Блещут бляхи, бляхи, бляхи,
возглашая матом благим:
«Люди — предки обезьян»,
«Губернатор — лесбиян»,
«Непечатное — в печать!»,
«Запретите запрещать!»

«Бог живет на улице Пастера, 18. Вход со двора».

Обожаю Гринич Вилидж
в саркастических значках.
Это кто мохнатый вылез,
как мошна в ночных очках?
Это Ален, Ален, Ален!
Над смертельным карнавалом,
Ален, выскочи в исподнем!
Бог — ирония сегодня.
Как библейский афоризм
гениальное: «Вались!»

Хулиганы? Хулиганы.
Лучше сунуть пальцы в рот,
чем закиснуть куликами
буржуазовых болот!

Бляхи по местам филейным
коллективным Вифлеемом
в мыле давят трепака —
«минн» около пупка.

AMERICAN BUTTONS

Buttons flash, buttons, buttons, buttons
shouting at the tops of their lungs
"Men are the ancestors of apes"
"Ronald Reagan is a lesbian"
"Fuck censorship"
"If it moves, fondle it"

GOD LIVES AT 18 PASTEUR ST.
REAR ENTRANCE PLEASE

I love Greenwich Village
with its sarcastic buttons.
Who's the shaggy one who showed up
cock & balls in dark glasses?
It's Allen, Allen, Allen!
Leap over Death's carnival,
Allen, in your underwear!
Irony is God today.
"Power to the People" is a holy slogan.

Better to stick your fingers in your mouth and whistle
than to be silent *booboisie.*

Button-stars of Bethlehem
on everybody's bottom,
mini-skirts on bellybuttons.

A wild girl agitator
winks from a dark corner
"Make love not war!"

Это Селма, Селма, Селма
агитирующей шельмой
подмигнула и — во двор:
«Мэйк лав, нот уор!»*

Бог — ирония сегодня.
Блещут бляхи над зевотой.
Тем страшнее, чем смешней,
и для пули — как мишень!

«Бог переехал на проспект Мира, 43.2 звонка».

И над хиппи, над потопом
ироническим циклопом
блещет Время, как значком,
округлившимся зрачком!

*Ах, Время,
сумею ли я прочитать, что написано в
                                    твоих очах,
мчащихся на меня,
                    увеличиваясь, как фары?
Успею ли оценить твою хохму?..*

*Ах, осень в осиновых кружочках...
Ах, восемь
подброшенных тарелочек жонглера,
                    мгновенно замерших в воздухе.
будто жирафа убежала,
                    а пятна от нее
                                    остались!..*

Удаляется жирафа
в бляхах, будто мухомор,
на спине у ней шарахнуто:
«Мэйк лав, нот уор!»

* «Твори любовь, а не войну!»

138

Irony is God today.
Buttons flash over yawns.
The funnier they are, the more terrifying
And like bullseyes for bullets.

GOD HAS MOVED TO 43 AVENUE OF PEACE.
RING TWICE.

And above the Hippies, —above the Flood
like an ironic Cyclops
Time flashes its button-eye!

TIME,
Can I read what's written in your eyes,
rushing at me—
          growing bigger and bigger, like headlights?
Can I see through your antics?

O autumn with round leaves
O eight plates
tossed up by a juggler
                    frozen for an instant in air,
as if a giraffe had run away,
                    and left its spots
                              behind!

The giraffe retreats
with a sacred mushroom-button on its bottom:
"Make Love Not War"

                    (translated by Lawrence Ferlinghetti)

ИСТОКИ

Меня тоска познанья точит.
и Беркли в сердце у меня.
Его студенчество — источник
безумства, света и ума.

А клеши спутницы прелестной
вниз расширялись в темноте —
как тени расширялись, если
источник света в животе.

SOURCES

I came to learn,
To explore the secrets of Berkeley,
To find in its students the sources
Of rebellion, light, and ideas.

But I was sidetracked by a coed's black bell-bottomed trousers,
Which flared out as shadow would flare out
If the source of light
Were centered in her belly.

(translated by William Jay Smith)

МОЛЧАЛЬНЫЙ ЗВОН

Их, наверно, тыщи — хрустящих лакомок!
Клесты лущат семечки в хрусте крон.
Надо всей Америкой
                              хрустальный благовест.
Так необычаен   молчальный звон.

Он не ради славы, молчальный благовест,
просто лущат пищу — отсюда он.
Никакого чуда, а душа расплакалась —
молчальный звон!..

Это звон молчальный таков по слуху,
будто сто отшельничающих клестов
ворошат волшебные погремухи
или затевают сорок сороков.

Птичьи коммуны, не бойтесь швабры!
Групповых ансамблей широк почин.
Надо всей Америкой — групповые свадьбы.
Есть и не поклонники групповщин.

Групповые гонки, групповые койки.
Тих единоличник во фраке гробовом.
У его супруги на всех пальцах —
                              кольца,
видно, пребывает
                    в браке групповом...

А по-над дорогой хруст серебра.
Здесь сама работа звенит за себя.
Кормят, молодчаги, детей и жен,
ну а получается
                    молчальный звон!

SILENT TINGLING

Must be thousands of sweet gourmets rustling through
leaf crowded branches, thrushes cracking seedling shells
all over America like crystalline carillon bells,
a really strange silent tingling.

Silent carillons, not to celebrate Main Street
but rustling up some food their only scene—
No miracle but millions of hungry souls
silently tingling.

This tingling silence heralds
an orgy of hermit thrushes eating,
like thousands of song-men's clapsticks clacking
or faraway Moscow's million bells
—some dream collective—generational vogue.

Thrush communes don't be afraid of the big Broom,
your flock continues an ancient tradition,
now all over America—collective marriage;
though some detractors put down your in-group, not big enough!

A silent Individualist in top hat & tails drest
coffinlike denounces your collective struggles in bed—
but his own wife wears rings on every finger,
as if she wound up in a group marriage.

This gentle gang's only enemy's insects,
cleaning up bark parasites—silently, silently—
Anybody can crush bones and oink louder
but can't beat this silent tingling.

Fast New York Sydney chicks—
thanks Brisbane birds & Chicago thrushes
for your own silent tingling—your cities' trees'
leaves tremble like golden curlicues on Byzantine crosses.

В этом клестианстве — антипод свинарни.
Чистят короедов — молчком, молчком!
Пусть вас даже кто-то

                      превосходит в звонарности,
но он не умеет

             молчальный звон!

Юркине ньюйорочки и чикагочки,
за ваш звон молчальный спасибо,

                 клесты.
Звенят листы дубовые,

          будто чеканятся
византийски вырезанные кресты.

В этот звон волшебный уйду от ужаса,
посреди беседы замру, смущен.
Будто на Владимирщине —

               прислушайся! —
молчальный звон...

Maybe someday our descendants
'll ask about this poet—What'd he sing about?
I didn't ring Halleluiah bells, I didn't clang leg-irons,
I was silently tingling.

(translated by Allen Ginsberg)

ЛОДКА НА БЕРЕГУ

Над лодкой перевернутою, ночью,
над днищем алюминиевым туга,
гимнастка, изгибая позвоночник,
изображает ручку утюга!

В сияньи моря северно-янтарном
хохочет, в днище впаяна, дыша,
кусачка, полукровочка, кентаврка,
ах, полулодка и полудитя...

Полуморская-полугородская,
в ней полуполоумнейший расчет,
полутоскует — как полуласкает,
полуутопит — как полуспасет.

Сейчас она стремглав перевернется.
Полузвереныш, уплывет — вернется,
по пальцы утопая в бережок...

Ужо тебе, оживший утюжок!

A BOAT ON THE SHORE

On the overturned boat in clear outline,
Taut, on its aluminum hull at night,
Is a gymnast who, arching back her spine,
Becomes the handle of a flat-iron.

In the North Sea's constant amber glitter
Like a pair of pliers, this half-caste, wild,
Centaur-like creature, welded to the hull
Is partly a boat and partly a child.

Half spirit of the city, half spirit of the sea,
She carries on this silly flirtation:
Half-sulking at first, and then half-friendly,
Will save you and then drop you back in the ocean.

She will of a sudden flip over and
Dart into the water, half-seal swim about;
Then return to burrow deep in the sand. . . .

Just wait, little iron, till you're ironed out!

(translated by William Jay Smith and Max Hayward)

РОЖДЕСТВЕНСКИЕ ПЛЯЖИ

Людмила,
            в сочельник,
                        Людмила,
                                    Людмила,
в вагоне зажженная елочка пляшет.
Мы выйдем у Взморья.
                        Оно нелюдимо.
В снегу наши пляжи!

В снегу наше лето.
                        Боюсь провалиться.
Под снегом шуршат наши тени песчаные.
Как если бы гипсом
                        криминалисты
следы опечатали.

В снегу наши августы, жар босоножек —
все лажа!
Как жрут англичане огонь и мороженое,
мы бросимся навзничь
                        на снежные пляжи.

Сто раз хоронили нас мудро и матерно,
мы вас эпатируем счастьем, мудрилы!..
Когда же ты встанешь,
                        останется вмятина —
в снегу во весь рост
                        отпечаток
                                    Людмилы.

Людмила,
            с тех пор в моей спутанной жизни
звенит пустота —
                        в форме шеи с плечами,

CHRISTMAS BEACHES

My darling
        Liudmila,
                on Christmas Eve,
                        my darling,
a lighted Christmas tree in the railway car does a dance.
Let's get off at the beach.
                No one there.
Our beaches snowed under
Our summer snowed under!
                I'm afraid I'll fall through.
Our sandy shadows stir under the snow
As if police had fixed our prints in plaster.

Our snowed-under Augusts, the heat of our feet—
all absurd!
And like Englishmen who gulp ice-cream on fire
we'll throw ourselves down together
                      on snowy sands.

Hundreds of times they've buried us
                with their so wise plaster castigations!
Wise men, our happiness bugs you.
And now when you get up, Liudmila,
                there'll be a hollow place,
a copy of you,
        lifesize
            in the snow!

Liudmila,
        my life's been so confused since then—
emptiness rings like a bell
                in the shape of a neck and shoulders,
with two empty hollows
              made by knees,
And like a chimney draft, it sucks me in.

и две пустоты —

                как колени оттиснуты,
и тянет и тянет, как тяга печная!

С звездою во лбу прибегала ты осенью
в промокшей штормовке.
Вода западала в надбровную оспинку.
(Наверно, песчинка прилипла к формовке.)

Людмилая-2, я помолвлен с двойняшками.
Не плачь. Не в Путивле.
Как рядом болишь ты,

                подушку обмявши,
и тень жалюзи

          на тебе,

             как тельняшка...
Как будто тебя

         от меня ампутировали.

With a star on your brow
                        you used to come running in Autumn,
your raincoat soaked through,
a raindrop in the small pockmark on your forehead.
(One grain of sand must have stuck in your mold.)

My double Liudmi-love, I'm betrothed to twins.
Don't cry. This isn't "Prince Igor."
Pressed against my pillow, you ache in me,
and the shadow of the shutters
                        lies upon you
                                    like a striped sailor's shirt
Cutting us apart.

(translated by Robert Bly and Lawrence Ferlinghetti)

МУРАВЕЙ

Он приплыл со мной с того берега,
заблудившись в лодке моей.
Не берут его в муравейники.
С того берега муравей.

Черный он, и яички беленькие,
даже, может быть, побелей...
Только он муравей с того берега,
с того берега муравей.

С того берега он, наверное,
как католикам старовер,
где иголки таскать повелено
остриями не вниз, а вверх.

Я б отвез тебя, черта беглого,
да в толпе не понять — кто чей.
Я и сам не имею пеленга
того берега, муравей.

Того берега, где со спелинкой
земляниковые бока...
Даже я не умею пеленга,
чтобы сдвинулись берега!

Через месяц на щепке, как Беринг,
доплывет он к семье своей,
но ответят ему с того берега:
«С того берега муравей».

ANT

He arrived with me from the other shore,
lost, having wandered onto my boat.
The ant heaps don't dig him.
He's an ant from the other shore.

A black ant—with such white eggs!
Maybe even whiter than . . .
But he's an ant from the other shore, you know,
he's an other-shore ant.

In his other-shoredness, the Catholics
see him as just a fundamentalist Orthodox ant.
The rule there is that all needles shall be carried
points-downward, not in the air.

I'd like to take you back with me, runaway brother,
but in this crowd you can't tell who belongs to which shore.
Brother ant, even I don't have the astrolabe
to find the way to that other shore.

The strawberries on that other shore
Have gotten too ripe and are turning.
Even if I had the astrolabe,
I couldn't make the shore come any closer.

After a month afloat like Captain Bering
the ant on his driftwood will soon reach his family.
They will answer him from the other shore:
"You are an ant from the other shore."

(translated by Robert Bly and Vera Dunham)

ДОНОР ДЫХАНИЯ

Так спасают автогонщиков.
Врач случайная, не ждавши «скорой помощи»,
с силой в легкие вдувает кислород —
рот в рот!
Есть отвага медицинская последняя —
без посредников, как жрица мясоедная,
рот в рот,
не сестрою, а женою милосердия
душу всю ему до донышка дает —
рот в рот,
одновременно массируя предсердие.

Оживаешь, оживаешь, оживаешь.
Рот в рот, рот в рот, рот в рот.
Из ребра когда-то созданный товарищ,
она нас из дыханья создает.

А в ушах звенит, как соло ксилофона,
мозг изъеден углекислотою.
А везти его до Кировских ворот!
(Рот в рот. Рот в рот).
Синий взгляд, как пробка, вылетит из-под
век, и легкие вздохнут, как шар летательный.
Преодолевается летальный
исход.

«Ты лети, мой шар воздушный, мой минутный!
Пусть в глазах твоих мной вдутый небосвод.
Пусть отдашь мое дыхание кому-то —
рот в рот...»

BREATH DONOR

This is how race-car drivers are saved.
No ambulance in sight,
A woman comes to the rescue,
forces air into the lungs,
mouth-to-mouth!

There's a kind of absolute courage
without medical help:
A pagan priestess,
not a Sister of Mercy but a Wife of Mercy,
is giving all herself to him,
mouth-to-mouth,
massaging his heart at the same time.

Come, come, come, come to!
mouth-to-mouth, mouth-to-mouth, mouth-to-mouth.
Made of our rib,
Now she makes life with her breath.

A brain eaten-out by carbon dioxide
rings in the ears
like a xylophone solo.
O if we can get him to the gates in time!
(Mouth-to-mouth, mouth-to-mouth.)

Like a cork a deep blue stare
pops out from under his eyelids
And his lungs expand like a balloon.
Death is defeated.

"Sail away, my balloon, mine for a moment!
Your eyes filled with the blue I breathed—
Give my breath to some other lover,
mouth-to-mouth . . ."

(translated by Lawrence Ferlinghetti)

СТЕКЛОЗАВОД

Сидят три девы-стеклодувши
с шестами, полыми внутри.
Их выдуваемые души
горят, как бычьи пузыри.

Душа имеет форму шара,
имеет форму самовара.
Душа — абстракт. Но в смысле формы
она дает любую фору!

Марине бы опохмелиться,
но на губах ее горит
душа пунцовая, как птица,
которая не улетит!

Нинель ушла от моториста.
Душа высвобождает грудь,
вся в предвкушенье материнства,
чтоб накормить или вздохнуть.

Уста Фаины из всех алгебр
с трудом две буквы назовут,
но с уст ее абстрактный ангел
отряхивает изумруд!

Дай дуну в дудку, постараюсь.
Дай гостю душу показать.
Моя душа не состоялась,
из формы вырвалась опять.

В век Скайлэба и Байконура
смешна кустарность ремесла.
О чем, Марина, ты вздохнула?
И красный ландыш родился.

AT THE GLASS-BLOWING FACTORY

Three young Venetian girls are sitting
with blowpipes in their mouths. Three souls,
each one blown through a pipe, now glisten
like three gall bladders from three bulls.

Some souls are spherical in shape;
others look more like samovars.
Although they *are* abstract, as far's
their form's concerned, they've got it made.

Marina'd like a morning snifter;
but perched upon her lips there glistens
a crimson soul, resembling
a bird refusing to take wing.

Ninel's walked out on her grease monkey.
Thanks to her soul, her bosom's freed
so as (when she becomes a mommy)
to heave great sighs and/or breast-feed.

Of all the algebraic symbols,
Fanny *might* know what two are called.
Yet from her lips, an abstract angel
lets drop a perfect emerald.

"Let *me* blow once! I'll do my best.
I'd like to let you see my soul."
Alas, it didn't pass the test:
again, it overflowed the mold.

Today, with Baikonur and Skylab,
such crude techniques arouse our mirth.
Marina, *what* set you to sighing,
thus bringing that red flower to birth?

Уходят люди и эпохи,
но на прилавках хрусталя
стоят их крохотные вздохи
по три рубля, по два рубля...

О чем, Марина, ты вздохнула?
Не знаю. Тело упорхнуло.
Душа, плененная в стекле,
стенает на моем столе.

Both individuals and eras
pass on; but their brief sighs are still
preserved in glassware shops, on sale
for ten or maybe twenty liras.

Marina, *what* set you to sighing?
I'll never know—you're dead and gone.
But on my desk, your soul—confined in
its glass integument—still moans.

(translated by Guy Daniels)

УЖЕ ПОДСНЕЖНИКИ

К полудню
или же поздней еще,
ни в коем случае
не ранее,
набрякнут под землей подснежники.
Их выбирают
с замираньем.

Их собирают
непоспевшими
в нагорной рощице дубовой,
на пальцы дуя
покрасневшие,
на солнцепеке,
где сильней еще
снег пахнет
молодой любовью.

Вытягивайте
потихонечку
бутоны из стручка
опасливо —
как авторучки из чехольчиков
с стержнями белыми
для пасты.

Они заправлены
туманом,
слезами
или чем-то высшим,
что мы в себе
        не понимаем,
не прочитаем,
но не спишем.

SNOWDROPS

About noon
or later
but certainly
no sooner
snowdrops will blossom underground.
With bated breath
you'll dig them out.

You will pick them
prematurely,
blowing on reddened
fingers
in the hot sunshine
of the oak grove on the hill,
where the snow even now
is more redolent
of young love.

You'll extract—
slowly—
carefully—
the buds from their pods
like ballpoint pens
from their casings,
white stems
made to hold ink.

They are seasoned
with mist,
with tears
or something deeper
within us
        which we do not understand,
and do not read
but do not write off.

Но где-то вы уже записаны,
и что-то послучалось
                        с вами
невидимо,
но несмываемо.
И вы от этого зависимы.

Уже не вы,
а вас собрали
лесные пальчики в оправе.
Такая тяга потаенная
в вас,
новорожденные змейки,
с порочно-детскою,
                        лимонною
усмешкой!

Потом вы их на шапку
                        сложите, —
кемарьте,
замерзнувшие, как ложечки,
серебряные
и с эмалью.

Когда же через час
                        вы вспомните:
«А где же?»
В лицо вам ткнутся
пуще прежнего
распущенные
                        и помешанные —
уже подснежники!

1968

But somewhere you're already noted down;
something has already happened to you
invisibly
and yet indelibly.
And you are linked to that.

For it's no longer you who pick
but you who are picked
by little woodland fingers.
There's such a secret lure
to those
small newborn snakes
with their perversely childlike
                                        lemony
smile.

Then you'll arrange them
                            on a hat—
in a daze—
frozen like silver
enameled
teaspoons.

And when, an hour later,
you suddenly ask:
where are they?
they'll spring at your face,
even further open
than before
                —madly open—
snowdrops already full-formed.

(translated by William Jay Smith and Nicholas Fersen)

1968

*   *   *

Нам, как аппендицит,
поудалили стыд.

Бесстыдство — наш удел.
Мы попираем смерть.
Ну, кто из нас краснел?
Забыли, как краснеть!

Сквозь толщи наших щек
не просочится свет.
Но по ночам — как шов,
заноет — спасу нет!

Я думаю, что Бог
в замену глаз и уш
нам дал мембрану щек,
как осязанье душ.

Горит моя беда,
два органа стыда —
не только для бритья,
не только для битья.

Спускаюсь в чей-то быт,
смутясь, гляжу кругом —
мне гладит щеки стыд
с изнанки утюгом.

Как стыдно, мы молчим.
Как минимум — схохмим.
Мне стыдно писанин,
написанных самим.

Далекий ангел мой,
стыжусь твоей любви
авиазаказной...
Мне стыдно за твои

SHAME

Our shame is cured, like the appendix,
  removed.

Now our problem is lack of shame.
Death is nothing.
Come on, who's even blushed?
No one knows how!

Light refuses to escape
through the flesh of our face!
But at night our faces
ache like sutures—nothing to do!

Maybe instead of ears
and eyes God just gave us a place
for our soul to live
in the muscles of our cheeks.

Those two things secrete shame,
I want them to burn!
Surely they're good for more
than shaving or slapping.

I go down into someone's life,
embarrassed, I look around—
shame, like a flat iron,
smooths my cheeks from inside.

We are ashamed to be silent.
What do we do—tell jokes.
I'm ashamed of the bits
of paper I've sent out myself.

My far-off angel, your
love by registered
air mail makes me ashamed.
Your tears that fall

соленые, что льешь.
Но тыщи раз стыдней,
что не отыщешь слез
на дне души моей.

Смешон мужчина мне
с напухшей тучей глаз.
Постыднее вдвойне,
что это в первый раз.

И черный ручеек
бежит на телефон
за все, за все, что он
имел и не сберёг,

за все, за все, за все,
что было и ушло,
что сбудется ужо,
и все еще — не все...

В больнице режиссер
чернеет с простыней.
Ладони распростер.
Но тыщи раз стыдней,

что нам глядит в глаза,
как бы чужие мы,
стыдливая краса
хрустальнейшей страны.

Застенчивый укор
застенчивых лугов,
застенчивая дрожь
застенчивейших рощ...

Обязанность стиха
быть органом стыда.

make me ashamed.
Here's what's more shameful:
On the bottom of my soul
you won't find any tears.

A man with his eyes puffed out like a heavy
cloud looks ridiculous to me.
Because it's for the first time
it's twice as shameful.

And a black stream
flows into the telephone
for all, all that he
had and didn't keep,

for everything, everything, everything
that has been and is gone,
that will happen somehow,
yet, not all of it. . . .

In the hospital a director
turns dark with his bedsheet.
His hands are thrown out.
Here's something more shameful than that:

that the calm beauty
of this most transparent of countries
looks us in the eye
as if we didn't belong to her.

Have you noticed how the shy
pastures look at us,
there's a shy trembling
in those deeply shy woods. . . .

What poetry ought to be
is
something that produces shame.

(translated by Robert Bly)

ЗАСУХА

В саду омывая машину,
к обочине перейду
и вымою ноги осине,
как грешница ноги Христу.

И ливень, что шел стороною,
вернется на рожь и овес.
И свет мою душу омоет,
как грешникам ноги Христос.

DRY SPELL

While washing the car in the open,
I move to one side, off the street,
and sprinkle the base of an aspen,
like the Magdalen washing Christ's feet.

The cloudburst, which had been moving southward,
will veer back, drenching oats, rye, and wheat;
and a clear light will lave my spirit,
just as Christ washed the sinners' feet.

(translated by Guy Daniels)

КРОМКА

Над пашней сумерки нерезки,
и солнце, уходя за лес,
как бы серебряною рельсой
зажжет у пахоты обрез.

Всего минуту, как, ужаля,
продлится тайная краса.
Но каждый вечер приезжаю
глядеть, как гаснет полоса.

Моя любовь передвечерняя,
прощальная моя любовь,
полоска света золотая
под затворенными дверьми.

1970

THE EDGE

Twilight over the field is blurred,
and the sun, setting beyond the forest,
lights up the edge of the plowed land
so it gleams like a silver rail.

Only a minute, like the sting of a bee,
will that secret beauty last.
But every evening I go to see
how the sliver of light fades away.

My early evening love,
my love, my farewell love,
a golden sliver of light
under closing doors.

(translated by Robert Ford)

1970

Есть русская интеллигенция.
Вы думали — нет? Есть.
Не масса индифферентная,
а совесть страны и честь.

Есть в Рихтере и Аверинцеве
земских врачей черты —
постолько интеллигенция,
поскольку они честны.

«Нет пороков в своем отечестве».
Не уважаю лесть.
Есть пороки в моем отечестве,
зато и пророки есть.

Такие, как вне коррозии,
ноздрей петербуржской взлет,
Николай Александрович Козырев —
небесный интеллигент.

Воюет с извечной дурью,
для подвига рождена,
отечественная литература —
отечественная война.

Какое призванье лестное
служить ей, отдавши честь:
«Есть, русская интеллигенция!
Есть!»

THE RUSSIAN INTELLIGENTSIA

The Russian intelligentsia lives.
You thought that it had perished, did you? . . .
Nor is it an amorphous mass
but our honor and our conscience, too.

Richter and Averintzev
are like doctors out in the country:
an intelligentsia exists
thanks to their simple honesty.

When they say a country can do no wrong,
I condemn such flattery.
My country has terrible problems
but also prophets who can see.

Immune to all corruption,
with his haughty Petersburg mien,
Nikolai Aleksandrovich Kozyrev
broods celestial on the scene.

Fighting eternal idiocy,
born to the greatest deeds there are,
the literature of Russia
conducts civil war.

How fine it is to serve it,
and saluting it, to aver:
"At your orders, Intelligentsia!
Long may you live! Yes, sir!"

(translated by William Jay Smith and Vera Dunham)

ПОРНОГРАФИЯ ДУХА

Отплясывает при народе
с поклонником голым подруга.
Ликуй, порнография плоти!
Но есть порнография духа.

Докладчик порой на лектории,
в искусстве силен как стряпуха,
раскроет на аудитории
свою порнографию духа.

В Пикассо ему все не ясно,
Стравинский — безнравственность слуха.
Такого бы постеснялась
любая парижская шлюха.

Подпольные миллионеры,
когда твоей родине худо,
являют в брильянтах и пернах
свою порнографию духа.

Конечно, спать вместе не стоило б...
Но в скважине голый глаз
значительно непристойнее
того, что он видит у вас...

Клеймите стриптизы экранные,
венерам закутайте брюхо.
Но все-таки дух — это главное.
Долой порнографию духа!

1974

PORNOGRAPHY OF THE MIND

Naked the woman dances in public
with her naked partner.
Hail to pornography of the flesh,
but beware pornography of the mind.

The lecturing official knows as much
about art as a short-order cook;
he reveals to his audience
the pornography of the mind.

To him Picasso makes no sense,
Stravinsky offends his ear;
any whore off the street
knows better.

When things go badly for the people,
you secret millionaires
parade in your sables and diamonds,
pornographers of the mind.

Naked lovemaking may be shameful indeed,
but more shameful
the naked eye
at the crack in the wall.

Denounce striptease on the screen,
Wrap up the bellies of Venuses;
But what matters is the mind—
Down with pornography of the mind.

(translated by William Jay Smith and Vera Dunham)

1974

ЛЕДОВЫЙ ЭПИЛОГ

Лед, лед растет неоплатимо,
вину всеобщую копя.
Однажды прорванный плотиной
лед выйдет из себя!
Вина людей перед природой,
возмездие вины иной,
Дахау дымные зевоты
и капля девочки одной
и социальные невзгоды
сомкнут над головою воды —
не Ной,
не Божий суд, а самосуд,
все, что надышано, накоплено,
вселенским двинется потопом.
Ничьи молитвы не спасут.

Вы захлебнетесь, как котята,
в свидетельствовании нечистот,
вы, деятели, коптящие
незащищенный небосвод!

Вы, жалкою толпой обслуживающие
                                       патронов,
свободы,
           гения и славы
                  палачи,
лед тронется
по-апокалиптически!

Увы, надменные подонки,
куда вы скроетесь, когда
потопом
сполощет ваши города?!

ICE BLOCK

Ice immeasurably forms, grows,
Amassing universal guilt
Till like a dam it breaks
And ice again will flow!

Over man's guilt before nature,
His retribution for other guilt,
Over the smoke of Dachau—
All society's ills—
Icy waters will close.
No Noah then—
No judgment but man's—
The sum of all that has breathed and grown
Will sweep away in universal flood.
And prayer will be vain.

Like kittens you'll drown—
While filthy waters testify—
You useless public figures
Who foul a defenseless sky.

You wretched pack of toadies,
Executioners
         of
            freedom,
                  genius, glory,
Ice will move
In an unmistakable apocalypse.

Ah, you arrogant scum,
Exploiters of labor,
Where will you hide that day
When in the rising flood
Your cities wash away?

Сполоснутые отечества,
сполоснутый балабол,
сполоснутое человечество.
Сполоснутое собой!

И мессиански и судейски
по возмутившимся годам
двадцатилетняя студентка
пройдет спокойно по водам.

Не замочивши лыжных корочек,
последний обойдет пригорочек
и поцелует, как детей,
то, что звалось «Земля людей».

Nations washed away,
Phony talkers washed away,
Mankind washed away—
Its own victim—washed away.

A judge, a messiah
Across those angry years,
Calmly upon the water,
A girl of twenty will stroll.

With her ski-boots dry, she,
Rounding the last promontory,
Will embrace, as one would a child,
Our human world.

(translated by William Jay Smith and Vera Dunham)

СКРЫМТЫМНЫМ

«Скрымтымным» — это пляшут омичи?
скрип темниц? или крик о помощи?
или у Судьбы есть псевдоним,
темная ухмылочка — скрымтымным?

Скрымтымным — то, что между нами.
То, что было раньше, вскрыв, темним.
«Ты-мы-ыы...» — с закрытыми глазами
в счастье стонет женщина: скрымтымным.

Скрымтымным — языков праматерь.
Глупо верить разуму, глупо спорить с ним.
Планы прогнозируем по сопромату,
но часто не учитываем скрымтымным.

«Как вы поживаете?» — «Скрымтымным...»
«Скрымтымным!» — «Слушаюсь. Выполним».

Скрымтымным — это не силлабика.
Лермонтов поэтому непереводим.
Вьюга безликая пела в Елабуге.
Что ей померещилось? — скрымтымным...

А пока пляшите, пьяны в дым:
«Шагадам, магадам, скрымтымным!»
Но не забывайте — рухнул Рим,
не поняв приветствия: «Скрымтымным».

1971

DARKMOTHERSCREAM

Darkmotherscream is a Siberian dance,
cry from prison or a yell for help,
or, perhaps, God has another word for it—
ominous little grin—darkmotherscream.

Darkmotherscream is the ecstasy of the sexual gut;
We let the past sink into darkmotherscream also.
You, we—oooh with her eyes closed
woman moans in ecstasy—darkmother, darkmotherscream.

Darkmotherscream is the original mother of languages.
It is silly to trust mind, silly to argue against it.
Prognosticating by computers
We leave out darkmotherscream.

"How's it going?" Darkmotherscream.
"Motherscream! Motherscream!"
               "OK, we'll do it, we'll do it."

The teachers can't handle darkmotherscream.
That is why Lermontov is untranslatable.
When the storm sang in Yelabuga,
What did it say to her? Darkmotherscream.

Meanwhile go on dancing, drunker and drunker.
"Shagadam magadam—darkmotherscream."
Don't forget—Rome fell
not having grasped the phrase: darkmotherscream.

(translated by Robert Bly)

1971

ЗВЕЗДА

Аплодировал Париж
в фестивальном дыме.
Тебе дали первый приз —
«Голую богиню».

Подвезут домой друзья
от аэродрома.
Дома нету ни копья.
Да и нету дома.

Оглядишь свои углы
звездными своими,
стены пусты и голы —
голая богиня.

Предлагал озолотить
проездной бакинец.
Ты ж предпочитаешь жить
голой, но богиней.

Подвернется, может, роль
с текстами благими.
Мне плевать, что гол король!
Голая богиня...

А за окнами стоят
талые осины
обнаженно, как талант, —
голая Россия!

И такая же одна
грохает тарелки
возле вечного огня
газовой горелки.

STAR

At the Paris Film Festival,
when the smoke of the session clears,
the Oscar of the day,
"The Naked Goddess," is yours.

At the airport your friends arrive
in a flivver to take you home;
but without a cent to your name,
you can scarcely call it home.

You inspect each crack and crevice
with the eyes of a new-born star.
The four walls that surround you
are like the "Goddess" bare.

A traveler in from Baku
wants to dip you in gold like tar.
You prefer to live on nude—
The Naked Goddess you are.

You do not give a damn
if a good role comes to you:
The King he has no clothes,
and the Goddess is Naked, too.

Outside your double windows
the thawing aspens rise,
and denuded like your talent
Naked Russia lies.

And there in your dingy kitchen
you clatter the plates at night
by the eternal light
of a wretched gas-fire.

И мерцает из угла
в сигаретном дыме —
ах, актерская судьба! —
Голая богиня.

And there in the corner glitters
in the smoke of her cigarette—
the destiny of an actress!—
"The Naked Goddess" yet.

(translated by William Jay Smith and Vera Dunham)

ЭЛЕГИЯ, НАПИСАННАЯ В ДОМИКЕ ОВИДИЯ

В пору, когда зацветает акация —
желтых измен семена неблагие, —
сердце сжимается, как от локации.
Это душевная аллергия.

В пору, когда отцветает провинция
белой пыльцой под строительной гирей,
я одобряю прораба провиденья,
но у меня на него аллергия.

Речи ли в клубе эрзацные слушаю,
или брожу почерневшею чащею,
или с холма загляжусь на цветущую
наших полей перспективу щемящую,
будто вдыхаю на косогоре
чьему-то ребенку грозящее горе.

Алигофрены цветут на плантациях.
В воздухе носятся мысли такие,
что, если бы воздухом этим питаться,
была бы у ангелов аллергия.

В пору, когда отвецает религия,
свадьбы летят — одуванчики Пасхи.
Религиозная аллергия
с платья трилистничком осыпается...

Не отцветай, моя тайная Муза!
Так же врасплох, как и в пору Вергилия,
Ты прибегаешь, целебно-дремуча!
Это предчувствует аллергия.

ELEGY WRITTEN IN THE LITTLE HOUSE
OF OVID

Now when the acacias are coming into bloom,
the sinister pollen of yellow betrayals,
my heart reacts like a radar antenna.
This is an allergy of the spirit.

Now that the provinces are losing their bloom
in a white dust under the wrecker's ball,
I assent to the builder's grand designs—
but I am allergic to him.

Whether I listen to ersatz speeches,
or wander alone through darkening woods,
or look down from a hill at the heart-wrenching
view of our flowering fields,
what I inhale is a sense of disaster—
like somebody threatening somebody's child.

Mental defectives bloom in their plantations,
expelling such thoughts into the air
that, if angels were to breathe it,
they would become allergic too.

Now that religion is no longer blooming,
weddings fly past like Easter dandelions,
scattering from pendant trefoils
allergy to religion.

My secret Muse, do not lose your bloom!
You'll come, I know, just as in Virgil's time
and take me by surprise, to soothe
and heal—this allergy tells me so.

(translated by Stanley Kunitz)

ОЗЕРО

Кто ты — непознанный Бог
или природа по Дарвину —
но я по сравненью с Тобой,
как я бездарен!

Озера тайный овал
высветлит в утренней просеке
то, что мой предок назвал
кодом нечаянным: «Господи...»

Господи, это же ты!
Вижу как будто впервые
озеро красоты
русской периферии.

Господи, это же ты
вместо исповедальни
горбишься у воды
старой скамейкой цимбальной.

Будто впервые к воде
выйду, кустарник отрину,
вместо молитвы Тебе
я расскажу про актрису.

Дом, где родилась она, —
между собором и баром...
Как ты одарена,
как твой сценарий бездарен!

Долго не знал о тебе.
Вдруг в захолустнейшем поезде
ты обернешься в купе:
Господи...

THE LAKE

Who are you? Unrecognized God
or simply Nature all so clear
to the Darwinian? Next to You
how stripped of talent I appear.

The morning light in the clearing
from the oval lake draws that which awed
my forebears, —what they casually,
intuitively addressed as "Lord."

O Lord, it truly now is You,
on whom for the very first time I gaze,
Your essence this lake's luminous haze
in the Russian provinces.

O Lord, it truly now is You,
met not in a dim confessional
but on a rickety slatted bench,
Your shadow hunched above the lake.

And to the lake's edge now I'll go
as for the first time through bright air,
and parting the reeds, in lieu of prayer,
tell of an actress that I know.

Tell of the house where she was born,
wedged between pub and cathedral,
and tell of her great gift and all—
and the wretched lines that she must learn.

I knew nothing at all of You:
As the train in the provinces raced ahead,
you turned to me your lovely head,
O Lord . . . I said . . . O Lord, it's You.

Господи, это же ты...
Помнишь, перевернулись
возле Алма-Аты?
Только сейчас обернулись.

Это впервые со мной,
это впервые,
будто от жизни самой
был на периферии.

Годы. Темноты. Мосты.
И осознать в перерыве:
Господи — это же ты!
Это — впервые.

O Lord, indeed, I know it's You:
Remember when the car overturned
there on the road near Alma-Ata
how to each other then we turned?

And for the first time now I see,
gazing out upon the lake:
It is as if to find you, Lord,
life sent me to its periphery.

Darkness. Darkness. Endless time . . .
Darkness. Bridges breaking through:
At the outer limit now of time,
Lord for the first time it is You.

(translated by William Jay Smith and Vera Dunham)

КНИЖНЫЙ БУМ

Попробуйте купить Ахматову —
вам букинисты объяснят,
что черный том ее агатовый
куда дороже, чем агат.

Кто некогда ее ругнули,
как к отпущению грехов,
стоят в почетном карауле
за томиком ее стихов.

«Прибавьте тиражи журналам» —
мы молимся книгобогам,
прибавьте тиражи желаньям
и журавлям.

Все реже в небесах бензинных
услышишь журавлиный зов.
Все монолитней в магазинах
сплошной Массивий Муравлев.

Страна желает первородства.
И может это добрый знак.
Ахматова не продается.
Не продается Пастернак.

BOOK BOOM

Just try to buy Akhmatova—
sold out. The booksellers say
her black, agate-colored tome
is worth more than agate today.

Those who once attacked her—
as if to atone for their curse—
stand, a reverent honor guard,
for a single volume of her verse.

"Print more copies of magazines,"
we beg of the great book gods.
"Give us more copies of our dreams,
release the cranes, vanished birds."

It's rare in our polluted skies
to hear the crane's lonely cries,
while every bookstore's lined with stacks
of monolithic published hacks.

The country demands its birthright,
and maybe that's as well:
Akhmatova will not sell out,
nor Pasternak, although he sell.

(translated by William Jay Smith and Vera Dunham)

БОБРОВЫЙ ПЛАЧ

Я на болотной тропе вечерней
встретил бобра. Он заплакал вхлюп.
Ручкой стоп-крана
                                торчал плачевно
красной эмали передний зуб.

Вставши на ласты, наморщась жалко
(у них чешуйчатые хвосты),
хлещет усатейшая русалка.
Ну, пропусти! Ну, пропусти!

(Метод нашли, ревуны коварные.
Стоит затронуть их закуток,
выйдут и плачут
                                пред экскаватором —
экскаваторщик наутек!

Выйдут семейкой и лапки сложат,
и заслонят от мотора кров.
«Ваша сила —
                                а наши слезы.
Рев — на рев!»)

В глазах старенького ребенка
слезы стоят на моем пути.
Ты что — уличная колонка?
Ну, пропусти, ну, пропусти!

Может, рыдал, что вода уходит?
Может, иное молил спасти?
Может быть, мстил за разор угодий!
Слезы стоят на моем пути.

Что же коленки мои ослабли?
Не останавливали пока
ни телефонные Ярославны,
ни бесноватые слезы царька.

THE BEAVER'S LAMENT

Strolling one evening through a swamp,
I met a beaver. He began to blubber.
His red enamel front tooth
stuck out—
        a pathetic emergency brake.

Rising on hind legs, wrinkling his brow
(they have scaly flat tails), he gushed forth,
mustachioed naiad of the north.
"Come on," I said, "now let me pass!"

(They have a way, the whining beasts:
As soon as you approach their lodge,
they confront the bulldozer
        and start to sob
till the driver takes pity and runs away.

An entire family comes forth, with clasped paws,
shielding their roof from destruction:
"Against your power
        we have tears—
our whine to match your engine's whine.")

Tears in the eyes of this aging child
stand in my way. What do you think you are?
Some old broken village pump?
Come on, please, let me pass.

Did he sob for the water that seeped away?
Or for something else he wished to save?
Did he sob to avenge his wasted land?
His tears were clearly in my way.

Why were my knees then giving way?
They have never given way so far—
not for widows weeping on the phone,
nor for the mad tears of an aging czar.

Или же заводи и речишник
вышли дорогу не уступать,
вынесли
       плачущий
           Образ Пречистый,
чтоб я опомнился, супостат?

Будьте бобры, мои годы и долы,
не для печали, а для борьбы,
встречные
       плакальщики
              укора,
будьте бобры,
          будьте бобры!

Непреступаемая для поступи,
непреступаемая стезя,
непреступаемая — о господи! —
непреступаемая слеза...

Я его крыл. Я дубасил палкой.
Я повернулся назад в сердцах.
Но за спиной моей новый плакал —
непроходимый другой в слезах.

1972

Or have all the creeks and streams
moved in to block the road,
carrying
      a weeping icon
             of the Mother of God
to bring their arch enemy to his senses?

Beavers, be with me in beastly places
in coming years,
         be brave, be sound,
you weeping
      and reproachful beavers.
Be beavers, beavers who stand your ground.

Let no one pass—block every step.
Let no one pass—cut off the road.
Let no one encroach upon these tears.
Let them be inviolable, O Lord. . . .

I cursed the beast. I beat him with my stick,
turned back from him in a fit of rage,
but behind me another beaver sprang up weeping—
another impassable barrier of tears.

        (translated by William Jay Smith and Vera Dunham)

1972

PART III

STORY UNDER FULL SAIL

(translated by Stanley Kunitz)

The literal English version of this poem was prepared by Vera Dunham, Maureen Sager, and Catherine Leach, a group of Slavists who undertook the task at the request of Andrei Voznesensky when he visited the United States in 1971. They are also responsible for the annotations and the Historical Note.

Поэму «Авось» я написал в Ванкувере.

Безусловно, в ванкуверские бухты заводил свои паруса Резанов и вглядывался в утренние холмы, так схожие с любезными его сердцу холмами сан-францисскими, где герой наш, «ежедневно куртизируя Гишпанскую красавицу, приметил предприимчивый характер ея», о чем откровенно оставил запись от 17 июня 1806 года.

Сдав билет на самолет, сломав сетку выступлений, под утро, когда затихают хиппи и пихты, глотал я лестные страницы о Резанове толстенного тома Дж. Ленсена, следя судьбу нашего отважного соотечественника.

Действительный камергер, создатель японского словаря, мечтательный коллега и знакомец Державина и Дмитриева, одержимый бешеной идеей, измученный бурями, добрался он до Калифорнии. Команда голодала. «Люди оцынжали и начали слягать. В полнолуние освежались мы найденными ракушками, а в другое время били орлов, ворон, словом ели, что попало...»

Был апрель. В Сан-Франциско, надев парадный мундир, Резанов пленил Кончу Аргуэльо, прелестную дочь коменданта города. Повторяю, был апрель. Они обручились. Внезапная гибель Резанова помешала свадьбе. Конча постриглась в монахини. Так появилась первая монахиня в Калифорнии.

За океаном вышло несколько восхищенных монографий о Резанове. У Брет Гарта есть баллада о нем.

Дописывал поэму в Москве.

В нашем ЦГИА хранится рукописный отчет Резанова, частью

IN PLACE OF A FOREWORD

I wrote this poem in Vancouver.

Without a doubt, Rezanov turned his sails into Vancouver's bays. And peered at the morning mountains so similar to his beloved San Francisco hills, where our hero "while daily courting a Spanish beauty, noted her venturesome character," as he frankly recorded under the date of June 17, 1806.

Toward morning, when the hippies and the pines calm down, having canceled my plane reservation and broken the thread of my public appearances, I devoured the enticing pages of G. Lensen's fat tome and followed the fate of our gallant countryman.

Chamberlain of the Russian Imperial Court, Ambassador to Japan, compiler of the first Japanese dictionary, visionary colleague and friend of Derzhavin and Dmitriev, a man possessed by a mad notion, wearied by storms, he battled his way to California. The crew was starving.

> The men were felled by scurvy. At full moon we refreshed ourselves with the mussels we found; at other times we killed eagles, crows; in a word, we ate anything we could lay our hands on. . . .

It was April. In San Francisco, attired in dress uniform, Rezanov captivated Concha Arguello (or Concepción), the enchanting daughter of the commandant of the town. I repeat: it was April. They became engaged. Rezanov's sudden death prevented the wedding. Concha took the veil. And became California's first nun.

Across the ocean, several rapturous monographs on Rezanov have appeared in print. Bret Harte wrote a ballad about him.

I finished my poem in Moscow.

Rezanov's manuscripts, published in part by Tikhmenev (St. Petersburg, 1863), are preserved in the State Central Historical

опубликованный у Тихменева (СПБ, 1863). Женственный, барочный почерк рисуют нам ум и сердце впечатлительное.

Какова личность, словесный жест! «Наконец являюсь я. Губернатор принимает меня с вежливостью, и я тотчас занял его предметом моим».

Слог каков! «...и наконец погаснет дух к важному и величественному. Словом: мы уподобимся обитому огниву, об который до устали рук стуча, насилу искры добьешься да и то пустой, которою не зажжешь ничего, но когда был в нем огонь, тогда не пользовались».

Как авакумовски костит он приобретателей: «Ежели таким бобролюбцам исчислить, что стоят бобры, то есть сколько за них людей перерезано и погибло, то может быть пониже бобровыя шапки нахлобучат!»

Как гневно и наивно в письме к царю пытается исправить человечество: «18 июля 1805 г. В самое тож время произвел я над привезенным с острова Атхи мещанином Куликаловым за бесчеловечный бой американки и грудного сына торжественный пример строгого правосудия, заковав сего преступника в железы...»

В поэму забрели два флотских офицера. Имена их слегка измененные. Автор не столь снедаем самомнением и легкомыслием, чтобы изображать лиц реальных по скудным сведениям о них и оскорблять их приблизительностью. Образы их, как и имена, лишь капризное эхо судеб известных. Да и трагедия евангелической женщины, затоптанной высшей догмой, — недоказуема, хотя и несомненна. Ибо неправа идея, поправшая живую жизнь и чувство.

Понятно, образы героев поэмы неадекватны прототипам.

Словом, если стихи обратят читателя к текстам и превоисточникам этой скорбной истории, труд автора был ненапрасен.

Archives. The delicate, baroque handwriting reveals a good mind and a sensitive heart.

What personality, self-esteem, verbal dash!

And then I appear. The Governor receives me with courtesy, and I engage him at once in a matter of concern to me.

What style!

. . . and at last the spirit will cease to respond to the great and the majestic. In a word, we shall become like a worn-down flint, which yields a spark only after our arms are ready to drop with the fatigue of striking it; but this spark is so faint it ignites nothing; yet when there was fire in the flint, we neglected to use it.

With what Avvakumian ire he belabors the accumulators of worldly goods:

If such lovers of beaver pelts would stop to reckon what beavers cost, that is, how many people have had their throats cut or in other ways perished for them, perhaps they would pull their beaver hats lower over their eyes!

With what anger and naïveté he attempts in a letter to the Tsar to set humanity aright:

July 18, 1805. At the same time I provided a solemn example of stern justice by putting in irons Kulikalov, a man of low estate, who had been brought over from Atka Island for the savage beating of a native woman and her infant son. . . .

Into the poem wandered two officers of the fleet. Why Khvostov and Davydov?

Given the scanty information at his disposal, the author is not so carried away by self-importance and frivolity as to attempt realistic portrayal and thus demean historical persons by a poor likeness. Their personalities, like their names, are but a capricious echo of the fates of great men. Furthermore, the tragedy, as I have conceived it, of sacred womanhood crushed by a "supreme idea" can neither be proved nor denied. But surely any dogma that overrides life and feeling is wrong.

If these verses lead readers of any land to the texts and original sources of this affecting tale, the author's labor will not have been in vain.

«А В О С Ь!»

ОПИСАНИЕ

в сентиментальных документах, стихах и молитвах
славных злоключений Действительного Камер-Герра
НИКОЛАЯ РЕЗАНОВА,
Доблестных Офицеров Флота Хвастова и Довыдова,
их быстрых парусников «Юнона» и «Авось»,
сан-францисского Коменданта Дон Хосе Дарно Аргуэльо,
любезной дочери его Кокчи
с приложением карты странствий необычайных.

STORY UNDER FULL SAIL

A DESCRIPTION

IN SENTIMENTAL DOCUMENTS, VERSE, AND PRAYERS
OF THE FAMED MISADVENTURES OF THE COURT
CHAMBERLAIN
NIKOLAI REZANOV,
THE VALIANT OFFICERS OF THE FLEET
KHVOSTOV AND DAVYDOV,
THEIR SWIFT SAILING SHIPS "JUNO" AND "PERCHANCE,"
THE COMMANDANT OF SAN FRANCISCO,
DON JOSÉ DARIO ARGUELLO,
HIS BELOVED DAUGHTER, CONCHA,
WITH A MAP OF THEIR UNCOMMON TRAVELS ATTACHED.

*«Но здесь должен я Вашему Сиятельству зделать испо-
ведь частных моих приключений. Прекрасная Консепсия
умножала день ото дня ко мне вежливости, разные инте-
ресные в положении моем услуги и искренность, начали
неприменно заполнять пустоту в моем сердце, мы ежечастно
зближались в объяснениях, которые кончились тем, что она
дала мне руку свою...»*

Письмо Н. Резанова Н. Румянцеву, 17 июня 1806 г.
(ЦГНА, ф. 13, с. 1 д. 687)

*«Пусть как угодно ценят подвиг мой, но при помощи
Божьей надеюсь хорошо исполнить его, мне первому из
Россиян здесь бродить так сказать по ножевому острию...»*

Н. Резанов — директорам русско-амер. компании
6 ноября 1805 г.
*«Теперь надеюсь, что «Авось» наш в Мае на воду спу-
щен будет...»*

от Резанова же 15 девраля 1806 г. Секретно-

"But at this point I must give your Excellency a true account of my personal adventures. Day after day the beautiful Concepción multiplied her courtesies toward me; imperceptibly, her sincerity and her different favors, valuable to me in my situation, began to fill the emptiness in my heart; we were drawn closer and closer by hours of mutual confidences, as a result of which she gave me her hand. . . ."

Letter from N. Rezanov to N. Rumyantsev, June 17, 1806. (Central State Historical Archives, Collection 13, file 687, page 1.)

"Let them judge my exploit as they will, but with God's help I hope to bring it to a successful conclusion because, apart from the common good, I see nothing and wish to see nothing. . . . I happen to be the first of the Russian nation to walk the razor's edge here, so to speak. . . ."

From N. Rezanov to the directors of the Russian-American Company, November 6, 1805.

"I now hope that our 'Perchance' will be launched in May. . . ."

Also from Rezanov, February 15, 1806. Marked Secret.

ВСТУПЛЕНИЕ

«Авось» называется наша шхуна.
Луна на волне, как сухой овес.
Трави, Муза, пускай худо,
но нашу веру зовут «Авось»!

«Авось» разгуляется, «Авось» вывезет,
гармонизируется Хавос.
На суше барщина и Фонвизины,
а у нас весенний девиз «Авось»!

Когда бессильна «Аве Мария»,
сквозь нас выдыхивает до звезд
атеистическая Россия
сверхъестественное «авось»!

Нас мало, нас адски мало,
и самое страшное, что мы врозь,
но из всех притонов, из всех кошмаров
мы возвращаемся на «Авось».

У нас ноль шансов против тыщи.
Крыш-ка!
Но наш ноль — просто красотища,
ведь мы выживали при «минус сорока».

PREFACE

Our schooner in the bay is called "Perchance."
The moon sprinkles oatmeal on the wave.
Chuck it up, Muse. Things may be bad now,
but we're ready to take a chance.

"Perchance" will put to sea, we'll make it
on a chance, tuned to Uncertainty!
Forced labor on dry land, and dreary shows,
but spring hauls our slogan up, "Perchance!"

"Hail Mary" died in our throat,
but through us godless Russia breathes,
as if in greeting to the Milky Way,
her transcendental word, "Perchance!"

We are few, we are damn few,
and worst of all we're separate and apart;
yet from all the hellholes, from all the nightmares,
we keep on struggling back, against the odds.

Our chances are zero in a thousand.
Cur-tains?
Oh . . . it's a beaut of a zero!
But we can live, we've learned, at forty below.

Довольно паузы. Будет шоу.
«Авось» отплытье провозгласил.
Пусть пусто у паруса за душою,
но пусто в сто лошадиных сил!

Когда ж, наконец, откинем копыта
и превратимся в звезду, в навоз —
про нас напишет стишки пиита
с фамилией, начинающейся на «Авось».

I. ПРОЛОГ

В Сан-Франциско ветра пиратствуют —
ЧП!
Доченька губернаторская
спит у русского на плече.

И за то, что дыханьем слабым
тельный крест его запотел,
Католичество и Православье,
вздев крыла, стоят у портьер.

Расшатываются устои.
Ей шестнадцать с позавчера,
с дня рождения удрала!
На посту Довыдов с Хвастовым
пьют и крестятся до утра.

II

ХВАСТОВ: «А что ты думаешь, Довыдов...»
ДОВЫДОВ: «О происхожденьи видов!»
ХВАСТОВ: «Да нет...»

Quit stalling. Get on with the show!
Our good ship toots her imminent departure.
What if the sails haven't a breath to their name?
That slack of theirs has horsepower to spare.

And when at last we flash our bellies up
and turn into a star or a heap of dung—
a sometime poet, bearing a chancy name,
will rhyme about us in his song.

PROLOGUE

I

In San Francisco winds are pirates.
Extra! Extra!
The governor's darling daughter's
head sleeps on a Russian's shoulder.

And because her light breath
has misted his baptismal cross,
Catholicism and Orthodoxy,
wings on point, guard the curtained door.

Custom and innocence are gone.
The day before yesterday, turned sixteen,
she fled her birthday feast.
Davydov and Khvostov, on watch,
drink and cross themselves till dawn.

II

KHVOSTOV: Davydov, what do you think about . . .
DAVYDOV: About the origin of species?
KHVOSTOV: No, not that. . . .

213

III

(*Молитва КОНЧИ АРГУЭЛЬО — БОГОМАТЕРИ*)

Плачет с сан-Францисской колокольни
барышня. Аукается с ней
Ярославна! Нет, Кончаковна —
Кончаковне посолоней!

«Укрепи меня, Матерь-заступница,
против родины и отца,
государственная преступница,
полюбила я пришлеца.

Полюбила за славу риска,
в непроглядные времена
на балконе высекла искру
пряжка сброшенного ремня.

И за то, что учил впервые
словесам ненашей страны,
что как будто цветы ночные,
распускающиеся в порыве,
ночью пахнут, а днем — дурны.

Пособи мне, как пособила б
баба бабе. Ах, Божья Мать,
ты, которая не любила,
как ты можешь меня понять!!

Как нища ты, людская вселенная,
в Боги выбравшая свои
плод искусственного осеменения,
дитя духа и нелюбви!

Нелюбовь в ваших сводах законочных.
Где ж исток!
Губернаторская дочь, Конча,
рада я, что сын твой издох!..»

CONCHA ARGUELLO'S PRAYER
TO THE MOTHER OF GOD

In a San Francisco bell tower
a girl in tears. Does Yaroslavna
call to her? No, it's Konchak's daughter,
long in exile by her husband's side.

"Bless me with strength, Mother-intercessor,
to stand against country and father.
I will not disown my treason, or this heart
or this flesh given to a stranger.

"Given in glory for what he dared for me . . .
(Time and darkness rolled like a tide
that night on the balcony; a spark flew
from his buckle, when he flung his belt aside.)

"And for teaching me to say
my first foreign words,
which, like night-flowers,
bursting into spray,
are fragrant in the dark and foul by day.

"Woman to woman,
help me. Oh, Mother of God,
you who have never loved,
how can you understand me?

"How desolate we creatures are
who chose for our God
the fruit of no human seed,
the child of Spirit and Denial!

"Denial stamps your codes of law.
Out of what fear?
I, Concha, the governor's daughter, am glad
your son died like a dog!"

И ответила Непорочная:
«Доченька...»

Ну, а дальше мы знать не вправе,
что там шепчут две бабы с тоской —
одна вся в серебре, другая —
до колен в рубашке мужской.

IV

ХВАСТОВ: А что ты думаешь, Довыдов...
ДОВЫДОВ: Как вздернуть немцев и пиитов!
ХВАСТОВ: Да нет... ДОВЫДОВ: Что деспоты
не создают условий для работы!
ХАСТОВ: Да нет...

V

(Молитва РЕЗАНОВА — БОГОМАТЕРИ)

«Ну, что тебе надо еще от меня!
Икона прохладна. Часовня тесна.
Я музыка поля, ты музыка сада,
ну что тебе надо еще от меня!

Я был не из знати. Простая семья.
Сказала: «Ты темен» — учился латыни.
Я новые земли открыл золотые.
И это гордыни твоей не цена!

Всю жизнь загубил я во имя Твоя.
Зачем же лишаешь последней услады!
Она ж несмышленыш и малое чадо...
Ну, что тебе мало уже от меня!»

And the Immaculate replied:
"Daughter dear . . ."

That's all we have a right to know of these
two women's anguished whisperings—
one dressed all in silver, the other
in a man's shirt down to her knees.

IV

KHVOSTOV: Davydov, what do you think about . . .
DAVYDOV: How to string up enemies and poets?
KHVOSTOV: No, not that. . . .
DAVYDOV: About the failure of despots to improve
            the workingman's lot?
KHVOSTOV: No, not that. . . .

V

REZANOV'S PRAYER TO THE MOTHER OF GOD

"Well, what more do you want from me?
The icon is cool. The chapel is small.
I am the music of the field; you are the music
                              of the garden.
You are the apple of hell, and unattainable.

"I was not high born. Of simple stock.
You said, 'You're ignorant'—I studied Latin.
I traveled far and wide, discovered golden lands.
Haven't I paid enough for your pride?

"I murdered love, and did it in your name.
You said, 'Be bold!'—I played with dynamite.
You said, 'Be first'—I won my fame.
Well, what more do you want from me?"

И вздрогнули ризы, окладом звеня.
И вышла усталая и без наряда.
Сказала: «Люблю тебя, глупый. Нет сладу.
Ну что тебе надо еще от меня!»

VI

ХВАСТОВ: А что ты думаешь, Довыдов...
ДОВЫДОВ: О макси-хламидах!
ХВАСТОВ: Да нет... ДОВЫДОВ: Дистрофично
безвластие, а власть катастрофична!
ХВАСТОВ: Да нет... ДОВЫДОВ: Вы надулись!
Что я и крепостник и вольнодумец!
ХВАСТОВ: Да нет. О бабе, о резановской.
Вдруг нас американцы водят за нос!
ДОВЫДОВ: Мыслю, как и ты, Хвастов, —
давить их, шлюх, без лишних слов.
ХВАСТОВ: Глядь! Дева в небе показалась,
на облачке. ДОВЫДОВ: Показалось...

VII

(Описание свадьбы, имевшей быть 1 апреля 1806 г.)

> «*Губернатор в доказательство
> искренности и с слабыми ногами
> танцевал у меня, и мы не щадили
> пороху ни на судне ни на кре-
> пости, гишпанские гитары сме-
> шивались с русскими песельни-
> ками. И ежели я не мог окончить
> женитьбы моей, то сделал конди-
> ционный акт...*»

Помнишь, свадебные слуги, после радужной севрюги,
апельсинами в вине обносили не!

Her garments trembled, the silver panels rang.
She came out weary, without her finery,
and said, "I love you, silly. There's no fighting it.
Well, what more do you want from me?"

VI

KHVOSTOV: Davydov, what do you think about . . .
DAVYDOV: About maxiskirts?
KHVOSTOV: No, not that. . . .
DAVYDOV: About anarchy being dystrophic and government
catastrophic?
KHVOSTOV: No, not that. . . .
DAVYDOV: You're sulking? Because I'm a free-thinker
who owns serfs?
KHVOSTOV: No, not that. About the woman, about Rezanov's
woman. You don't suppose the Americans are
giving us the runaround?
DAVYDOV: I'm of the same mind as you, Khvostov—squash
them, the whores, and be done with it.
KHVOSTOV: Look! I see the Virgin in the sky on a puff
of cloud.
DAVYDOV: You're seeing things. . . .

VII

(*Description of a wedding, which was to have taken place on
April 1, 1806*)

"*In spite of his weak legs the governor, as proof of his
sincerity, danced as my guest, and no gunpowder was spared
either on the ship or in the fortress; Spanish guitars mixed
with Russian singers. And even though I could not complete
the marriage rites, I was punctilious in my prenuptial be-
havior. . . .*"

Do you remember the wedding servants
conveying the iridescent sturgeon, and afterward
the oranges in wine—though it never came to pass?

219

как лиловый поп в битловке, под колокола былого,
кольца, тесные с обновки с имечком на тыльной стороне, —
нам примерил не!

а Довыдова с Хвастовым, в зал обеденный с восторгом
        впрыгнувших на скакуне, —
выводили не!

а мамаша, удивившись, будто давленые вишни
        на брюссельской простыне, озадаченной родне, —
предьявила не!

(лейтенантик Н
застрелился не)

а когда вы шли с поклоном, смертно-бледная мадонна
        к фиолетовой стене
отвернулась не!

Губернаторская дочка,
где те гости! Ночь пуста.
Перепутались цепочкой
два нательные креста.

АРХИВНЫЕ ДОКУМЕНТЫ,
ОТНОСЯЩИЕСЯ К ДЕЛУ РЕЗАНОВА Н. Н.

(Комментируют арх. крысы — игреки и иксы)

№ 1.

*«...но имя Монарха нашего более благословляться будет,
когда в счастливые дни его свергнут Россияне рабство чуж-
дым народам... Государство в одном месте избавляется*

The lilac priest in a Nehru jacket, to an old-time bell,
trying on our fingers those tight new rings
with our names engraved on the skinside—though it never
                                    came to pass?

And Davydov and Khvostov in exaltation leaping
into the banquet hall astride a steed
and being escorted out—though it never came to pass?

And Mamá, bewildered, presenting
to puzzled relatives what looked like crushed cherries
on a Brussels sheet—though it never came to pass?

(The puny Lieutenant X
shooting himself—though it never came to pass.)

And the Madonna, deathly pale,
as you approached to kneel,
turning her face to the violet wall—though it never
                                    came to pass?

Governor's daughter!
Where are those guests? The night is empty.
The chains of two baptismal crosses
hang in a tangle.

ARCHIVAL DOCUMENTS RELATING TO
THE AFFAIRS OF
REZANOV, N. P.

[Comments by archival rats—Y's and X's]

NO. 1

". . . but the name of our Monarch will be all the more blessed
if, in the beneficent days of his reign, the Russians will throw off
their bondage to alien peoples. . . . The Empire rids itself of*

вредных членов, но в другом от них же получает пользу и
ими города создает...»

Н. Резанов — Н. Румянцеву

№ 2. ВТОРОЕ ПИСЬМО РЕЗАНОВА — И. И. ДМИТРИЕВУ

Любезный Государь Иван Иваныч Дмитриев,
оповещаю, что достал
тебе настойку из термитов.
Душой я бешено устал!

Чего ищу! Чего-то свежего!
Земли старые — старый сифилис.
Начинают театры с вешалок.
Начинаются царства с виселиц.

Земли новые — табула раза.
Расселю там новую расу —
Третий Мир — без деньги и петли,
ни республики, ни короны!
Где земли золотое лоно,
как по золоту пишут иконы,
будут лики людей светлы.

Был мне сон, дурной и чудесный.
(Видно, я переел синюх.)
Да, случась при Дворе, посодействуй —
на американочке женюсь...

ЧИН ИКС:

«А вы, Резанов,
из куртизанов!
Хихикс...»

№ 3. ВЫПИСКА ИЗ ИСТОРИИ гг. ДОВЫДОВА И ХВАСТОВА

Были петербуржцы — станем сыктывкарцы.
На снегу дуэльном — два костра.

criminal members at home, but derives benefit from them else-
where and employs them for building cities. . . ."

N. Rezanov to N. Rumyantsev

NO. 2. REZANOV'S SECOND LETTER TO I. I. DMITRIEV

My Dear Sir, Ivan Ivanych Dmitriev,
this is to tell you of my success
in acquiring for you some extract of termites.
My soul is racked with weariness!

What am I looking for? Something unspoiled!
Old lands—they're plagued with syphilitic rot.
Operas begin with the coat hanger,
and kingdoms with the hangman's knot.

New lands—*tabula rasa.*
There I'll settle a new race—
a Third World—without dollars or noose,
neither republic nor crown!—
lands of a beauty untold,
where faces in a crowd will shine
like icons painted on gold.

I had a dream, so full of wonders and forebodings
(could be those magic mushrooms that I tried).
Oh yes, when you're at court, say a good word for me—
the girl's American, and she's to be my bride. . . .

THE OFFICIAL X

"And you, Rezanov,
a gentleman of the court!
Heh-heh-x . . ."

NO. 3. EXCERPTS FROM THE STORY OF THE GENTLEMEN
DAVYDOV AND KHVOSTOV

Deuce of hearts turned up.
  On the snowy dueling field—two bonfires.

Одного — на небо, другого — в карцер!
После сатисфакции — два конца!
Но пуля врезалась в пулю встречную.
Ай да Довыдов и Хвастов!
Враги вечные на братство венчаны.
И оба — к Резанову, на Дальный Восток...

ЧИН ИГРЕК:

«Засечены в подпольных играх».

ЧИН ИКС:

«Но государство ценит риск».

«15 февраля 1806 г. Объясняя вам многие характеры, приступлю теперь к прискорбному для меня описанию г. Х......., главного действующого лица в шалостях и вреде общественном и столь же полезнаго и любезнаго человека, когда в настоящих он правилах... В то самое время покупал я судно Юнону и сколь скоро купил, то зделал его начальником, и в то же время написал к нему Мичмана Давыдова. Вступя на судно, открыл он то пьянство, которое три месяца к ряду продолжалось, ибо на одну свою персону, как из счета его в заборе увидите, выпил 9½ ведр французской водки и 2½ ведра крепкаго спирту кроме стпусков другим и, словом, споил с кругу корабельных, подмастерьев, штурманов и офицеров. Беспросыпное его пьянство лишило его ума, и он всякую ночь снимается с якоря, но к счастью, что матросы всегда пьяны...»

(Из Второго секретного письма Резанова)

«17 июня 1806 г. Здесь видел я опыт искусства Лейтенанта Хвостова, ибо должно отдать справедливость, что одною его решимостью спаслись мы, и столько же удачно вышли мы из мест, каменными грядами окруженных».

Резанов — министру коммерции

One man—to heaven, the other—to the brig!
  After satisfaction—two separate endings!
But bullet tore into oncoming bullet.
  Bravo, Davydov and Khvostov!
Two sworn enemies wedded in brotherhood,
  and to Rezanov, to the Far East . . .

THE OFFICIAL Y

"Caught at forbidden games."

THE OFFICIAL X

"But the Empire values risk."

February 15, 1806. "In giving you an account of various personalities, I shall now proceed with the painful description of Mr. Kh—— who is a leading figure in pranks and public mischief and at the same time a useful and obliging man when conducting himself properly. . . . When I was buying the ship 'Juno,' I put him in charge, and also assigned Ensign Davydov to him. On taking command of the ship, he commenced a drinking bout, which continued for three months in a row; as you will see from his stores account, he drank by himself 9½ ten-quart measures of French vodka and 2½ of strong spirits in addition to what was issued to others, and, in a word, turned the seamen, apprentices, helmsmen, and officers into drunkards. His constant sodden state has caused him to lose his reason and every night he weighs anchor, but luckily the sailors are always drunk. . . ."

(*From Rezanov's second secret letter*)

June 17, 1806. "Here I witnessed an instance of Lieutenant Khvostov's skill; for, in all fairness, we were saved by nothing other than his bold judgment, and succeeded in getting out of an area bounded by rocky ridges."

(*Rezanov to the Minister of Commerce*)

225

РАПОРТ

Мы — Довыдов и Хвастов,
оба лейтенанты.
Прикажите — в сто стволов
жахнем латинянам!

«Стоп, Довыдов и Хвастов!» —
«Вы мягки, Резанов». —
«Уезжаю. Дайте штоф.
Вас оставлю в замах».

В бой, Довыдов и Хвастов!
Улетели. Рапорт:
«Пять восточных островов
Ваши, Император!»

«Я должен отдать справедливость искусству гг. Хвостова и Давыдова, которые весьма поспешно совершили рейсы их...»

«18 октября 1807 г. Когда я взошел к Капитану Бухарину, он, призвав караульного унтер-офицера, велел арестовать меня. Ни мне ни Лейтенанту Хвостову не позволялось выходить из дому и даже видеть лицо какого-либо смертного... Лейтенант Хвостов впал в опасную горячку.

Вот картина моего состояния! Вот награда, есть ли не услуг, то по крайней мере желания оказать оные. При сравнении прошедшей моей жизни и настоящей сердце обливается кровью и оскорбленная столь жестоким образом честь заставляет проклинать виновника и самую жизнь.

Мичман Давыдов».

(Выписка из «Донесения Мичмана Давыдова на квартире уже под политическим караулом»)

We—Davydov and Khvostov,
both of us lieutenants—
request permission to smash the Japs
with a hundred cannon.

"Stop, Davydov and Khvostov!"—
"You're soft, Rezanov, soft!"
"I'm going. Break open a bottle.
I leave you in charge."

To battle, Davydov and Khvostov!
Away they flew. Report:
"Five eastern isles are yours,
Your Imperial Majesty!"

"In all fairness I must acknowledge the skill of Khvostov and Davydov, who made their runs with great dispatch. . . ."

October 18, 1807. "When I entered Captain Bukharin's quarters, he, having summoned a petty officer on duty, ordered him to arrest me. Neither I nor Lieutenant Khvostov was allowed to leave our respective quarters, nor even to see the face of any mortal soul. . . . Lieutenant Khvostov fell ill with a dangerous fever.

"Picture my condition! This was my reward, if not for services, then at least for a desire to render the same. When I compare my past life with the present, my heart bleeds, and my honor, offended in a manner so cruel, drives me to curse the one responsible and even life itself. . . ."

Ensign Davydov

(An excerpt from the "Report of Ensign Davydov, already confined to quarters under political arrest.")

227

№ 4. РЕЗАНОВ — И. И. ДМИТРИЕВУ

Зрю тысячу чудес. Из тысячи
Вам посылаю круг мистический:
из Тьмы рождаясь, Жизнь сия
вновь канет в Тьму небытия...

№ 5. МНЕНИЕ КРИТИКА ЗЕТА:

От этих модернистских оборотцев
Резанов ваш в гробу перевернется!

МНЕНИЕ ПОЭТА

Перевернется, — значит, оживет.
Живи, Резанов! «Авось», вперед!

№ 6. ЧИН ИГРЕК:

Вот панегирик:

*«Николай Резанов был прозорливым политиком. Живи
Н. Резанов на 10 лет дольше, то, что мы называем сейчас
Калифорнией и Американской Британской Колумбией, были
бы русской территорией».*

Адмирал Ван Дерс (США)

ЧИН ИКС: Сравним
что говорит нам Головнин:

*«Сей г. Резанов был человек скорый, горячий, затейливый
писака, говорун, имеющий голову более способную создавать
воздушные замки в кабинете, нежели к великим делам,
происходящим в свете...»*

Флота Капитан 2-го ранга и кавалер В. М. Головнин

NO. 4. REZANOV TO I. I. DMITRIEV

I behold a thousand miracles, out of which
I send you one mystic circle:
born of Darkness, this Life will revert
to Nothingness and Night.

NO. 5. THE OPINION OF CRITIC Z

These modernistic turns of phrase
will make your Rezanov turn in his grave!

THE OPINION OF THE POET

If he turns—he'll be restored.
Live, Rezanov! Onward, "Perchance"!

NO. 6. THE OFFICIAL Y

Here is a panegyric:

*"Rezanov's greater schemes have since become more definitely
known, and no one that has studied his life and character can
doubt that, had he lived ten years longer, what is now the
Western section of the United States, as well as British Columbia,
would be Russian territory."*

Gertrude Atherton

THE OFFICIAL X

Now let's see what Golovnin tells us:

*"This Rezanov was a quick, impetuous man, a fanciful pen-
wielder, a tongue-wagger who had more talent for building castles
in the air than for real affairs of great import. . . ."*

V. M. Golovnin, Lieutenant-Commander, Decorated

229

ЧИН ИКС:

«А вы, Резанов,
пропили замок.
Вот Иск».

№ 7. ИЗ ПИСЬМА РЕЗАНОВА — ДЕРЖАВИНУ

Тут одного гишпанца угораздило
по-своему переложить Горация.
Понятно, это не Державин,
но любопытен по терзаньям:

«Я памятник себе воздвиг чудесный вечный.
Увечный
наш бренный разум цепляется за пирамиды, статуи,
                                    памятные места —
тщета!
Тыща лет больше, тыща лет меньше — но далее ни черта!

Я — последний поэт цивилизации.
Не нашей, римской, а цивилизации вообще.
В эпоху духовного кризиса и цифиризации
культура — позорнейшая из вещей.

Позорно знать неправду и не назвать ее,
а назвавши, позорно не искоренять,
позорно похороны называть свадьбою,
да еще кривляться на похоронах.

За эти слова меня современники удавят.
А будущий афро-евро-америко-азиат
с корнем выроет мой фундамент,
и будет дыра из планеты зиять.

И они примутся доказывать, что слова мои были вздорные.
Сложат лучшие песни, танцы, понапишут книг...
И я буду счастлив, что меня справедливо вздернули.
Вот это будет тот еще памятник!»

"And you, Rezanov,
drank away the castle.
Here's the bill of particulars."

NO. 7. FROM A LETTER OF N. REZANOV TO G. DERZHAVIN

A Spaniard whom I've met aspires—the Lord knows why—
to better Horace at his game.
Of course he's no Derzhavin,
but there's something strangely desperate in his lines:

"I built myself a rare and lasting monument.
Consider this frail
and damaged mind groping for statues, forums, pyramids . . .
All is vanity!

"A thousand years more or a thousand less, then—*nada!*
I am the last poet of civilization,
not ours, not Roman, but everyman's.
In a sick age where souls are numbers
culture is the worst obscenity.

"It's shameful to spot a lie and not to name it,
shameful to name it and then to shut your eyes,
shameful to call a funeral a wedding
and play the fool at funerals besides.

"For that my confreres will do me in,
and then the eurafro-amerasian man-to-come
will yank my pedestal up by the roots,
leaving a gaping hole in the planet.

"And they'll set about proving my words were nonsense,
outdo my songs and dances, pile book on book . . .
And I shall rejoice for being strung up justly.
That will be a real monument!"

231

«16 августа 1804 г. Я должен так же Вашему Император-
скому Величеству представить замечания мои о приметном
здесь уменьшении народа. Еще более препятствует размно-
жению жителей недостаток женского полу. Здесь теперь
более нежели 30-ть человек по одной женщине. Молодые
люди приходят в отчаянье, а женщины разными по нужде
хитростями вовлекаются в распутство и делаются к дето-
рождению неспособными».

(Из письма Н. Резанова Императору)

ЧИН ИКС:

«И ты, без женщин забуревший,
на импорт клюнул зарубежный!!
Раскис!»

№ 9

«Предложение мое сразило воспитанных в фанатизме
родителей ея, разность религий, и впереди разлука с до-
черью было для них громовым ударом».

Отнесите родителям выкуп
за жену:
макси-шубу с опушкой из выхухоля,
Фасон «бабушка-инженю»,

Принесите кровать с подзорами,
и, как зрящий сквозь землю глаз,
принесите трубу подзорную
под названием «унитаз»

(если глянуть в ее окуляры,
ты увидишь сквозь шар земной
трубы нашего полушария,
наблюдающие за тобой),

August 16, 1804. "Unalaska Island. It is also my duty to report to your Imperial Majesty my observations concerning the noticeable decrease in population here. The paucity of females prevents any increase in population. There are now more than thirty men for every woman here. Young men despair, and women are inevitably misled into wantonness and rendered incapable of childbearing."

(*From N. Rezanov's letter to the Emperor*)

THE OFFICIAL X

"And you, grown horny without women,
snapped at a foreign import?!
Gone soft!"

NO. 9

"My proposal came as a blow to her parents, who had been reared in fanaticism; the difference in religion and the prospect of separation from their daughter struck them like a thunderbolt."

Take the bride-price
to the parents—
a maxi fur-coat trimmed with muskrat,
"granny-ingenue" style.

Bring in the canopied bed
and a spy-glass
trademarked "Sanitas"
that can penetrate solid earth

(if you peer into its eye-piece
you'll observe, through the globe,
the bowls of our hemisphere
staring back).

принесите бокалы силезские
из поющего хрусталя,
ведешь влево — поют «Марсельезу»,
ну а вправо — «Храни короля»,

принесите три самых желания,
что я прятал от жен и друзей,
что угрюмо отдал на заклание
авантюрной планиде моей!..

Принесите карты открытий,
в дымке золота как пыльца,
и, облив самогоном, —
сожгите
у надменных дверей дворца!

«...они прибегнули к Миссионерам, те не знали, как решиться, возили бедную Консепсию в церковь, исповедовали ее, убеждали к отказу, но решимость с обеих сторон наконец всех успокоила. Святые отцы оставили разрешению Римского Престола, и я принудил помолвить нас, на что соглашено с тем, чтоб до разрешения Папы было сие тайною».

№ 10. ЧИН ИКС:

«Еще есть образ Божьей Матери,
где на эмальке матовой
автограф Их-с...»

«Я представлял ей край Российской посуровее и притом во всем изобильной, она была готова жить в нем...»

Bring in the Silesian goblets
of singing crystal, whose rim,
rubbed leftward, intones the "Marseillaise,"
rightward, "God Save the King."

Bring in those same three wishes,
hidden from wives and friends,
that I grimly offered in blood sacrifice
to my tricky fate! . . .

Bring in the maps of discoveries
hazed with gold, like pollen;
drench them in home brew,
and burn them
by the haughty palace gates!

". . . they had resort to the Missionaries, but the latter did not
know what course to pursue; they took poor Concepción to
church, confessed her, urged her to refuse me; but the determina-
tion we both displayed finally wore them down. The holy fathers
left the matter to the decision of the Vatican, and I forced them
to betroth us. They agreed to the betrothal, with the understanding that it would remain secret, pending Papal consent."

NO. 10. THE OFFICIAL X

"There still exists a picture of the Mother of God
with Our Lady's autograph
on its frosted enamel. . . ."

"I spared no words in presenting Russia to her as a bleak
country and at the same time all-bountiful; she was prepared to
live there. . . ."

№ 11. РЕЗАНОВ — КОНЧЕ

Я тебе расскажу о России,
где злодействует соловей,
сжатый страшной любовной силой,
как серебряный силомер.

Там храм Матери Чудотворной.
От стены наклонились в пруд
белоснежные контрофорсы,
будто лошади воду пьют.

Их ночная вода поила
вкусом чуда и чабреца,
чтоб наполнить земною силой
утомленные небеса.

Через год мы вернемся в Россию.
Вспыхнет золото и картечь.
Я заставлю, чтоб согласились
царь мой, Папа, и твой отец!

VIII

(В сенате)

Восхитились. Разобрались. Заклеймили.
Разобрались. Наградили. Вознесли.
Разобрались. Взревновали. Позабыли.
Господи благослови!
А Довыдова с Хвастовым посадили.

IX

(Молитва БОГОМАТЕРИ — РЕЗАНОВУ)

Светлый мой, возлюбленный, студится
тыща восемьсотая весна!

I shall tell you about Russia
where the nightingale sings his head off
gripped in the crushing vise of love
like a silver compression gauge.

I know a church there of the Miraculous Mother.
From its walls snow-white buttresses
bend to the pond,
drinking water like horses.

The nightwater offers them
its tang of miracle and thyme,
till the exhausted skies brim
with the potency of earth.

Next year we'll go home to Russia.
Gold and lead will flash.
I shall wring consent
from my Tsar, the Pope, your father!

VIII

In the Senate

They were fascinated. Pondered. Branded him.
Pondered. Rewarded him. Exalted him.
Pondered. Burned with jealousy. Forgot him.
God bless us all!
And Davydov and Khvostov?—
They went to the lockup.

IX

MOTHER OF GOD'S PRAYER TO REZANOV

My shining one, my beloved,
the one-thousand-eight-hundredth spring is chill!

Матерь от Любви Своей Отступница,
я перед природою грешна.

Слушая рождественские звоны,
думаешь, я радостна была!
О любви моей незарожденной
похоронно бьют колокола.

Надругались. А о бабе позабыли.
В честь греха в церквах горят светильни.
Плоть не против Духа, ибо дух —
то, что возникает между двух.

Тело отпусти на покаяние!
Мои церкви в тыщи киловатт
загашу за счастье окаянное
губы в табаке поцеловать!

Бог, Любовь Единая в двух лицах,
воскреси любою из марусь...
Николай и наглая девица,
вам молюсь!

Э П И Л О Г

Спите, милые, на шкурах росомаховых.
Он погибнет в Красноярске через год.
Она выбросит в пучину мертвый плод,
станет первой сан-францисскою монахиней.

A Mother, and Apostate of My Love,
I have sinned against nature.

Do you think I rejoiced,
listening to the Christmas bells?
The bells toll
for my unbegotten love.

They violated me. Forgot I was womanish.
My sin pours oil in every votive lamp.
Flesh is not against Spirit; out of two—
Spirit is born.

Let my flesh go in peace!
Put out the lights
        in my thousand-kilowatt churches! . . .
Let me taste the profane joy
        of tobacco-flecked lips!

God, who is Love, one in two persons,
resurrect me—through any Mary.
Nikolai and careless wench,
I pray to you.

X

EPILOGUE

Sleep, my dears, on your wolverine pelts.
Next year at Krasnoyarsk he'll die alone.
She'll cast her stillborn into the deep
and become San Francisco's first nun.

239

AN HISTORICAL NOTE

When Andrei Voznesensky was in Vancouver in the early spring of 1971 he was presented with a copy of George A. Lensen's excellent account of Russian expansion in the North Pacific from the seventeenth to the late nineteenth century. The book, *The Russian Push Toward Japan,* * made an impression on the poet; in particular his imagination was touched by the personality and fate of one of the men in the forefront of Russia's march toward the Pacific—Nikolai Petrovich Rezanov.

Scion of an impoverished aristocratic family, Rezanov was forced to make a career for himself both at the Russian Imperial Court and in the world of trade and commerce. In five dazzling years he rose from guardsman in one of the elite regiments to captain of the guards at the court of Catherine the Great. Fifteen more years saw him reach the height of his career as Chamberlain of His Imperial Majesty, Alexander I, and majority stockholder and chairman of the board of directors of the Russian-American Company, the key instrument of Russian policy in the Pacific.

Energetic, intelligent, and enterprising, "one of the handsomest men in Europe,"† Rezanov was named Ambassador to Japan in 1803. He spent several fruitless months attempting to set up trade relations with the Japanese, partly to secure supplies for the struggling settlements of Russian fur traders in Alaska and the Aleutians, partly to obtain for Russia such oriental luxuries as silk, tea, and porcelain. But the Japanese thought little of the Russian proposals and were blunt in their reply to the Tsar's envoy. Their message to him concluded:

> Thus it is our government's will not to open this place; do not come again in vain. You must sail home quickly.‡

* George Alexander Lensen, *The Russian Push Toward Japan: Russo-Japanese Relations, 1697–1875* (Princeton: Princeton University Press, 1959).

† Gertrude Atherton, "Nikolai Petrovich Rezanov," *The North American Review*, Vol. 189 (January–June, 1909), p. 653.

‡ Lensen, p. 155.

Rezanov was shocked by the arrogance of the Japanese and outraged by their rejection of the Tsar's offer of friendship and commerce.

On April 30, 1805, he left the rockbound shores of Japan and traveled north to Okhotsk, and from there set off on a tour of inspection of the Company settlements on the Aleutian Islands. He spent the winter of 1805–6 in Sitka, known in those days as Novo-Arkhangelsk, and, on the eighth of March, 1806, set sail for San Francisco on the sloop *Juno* in the hope of making commercial agreements with the Spanish colonies in California.

The ship and its cargo had been purchased in Sitka from a Boston trader, Captain D'Wolf, and was under the command of a young Russian naval officer, Lieutenant Nikolai Aleksandrovich Khvostov. Also on board was Ensign Gavrilo Ivanovich Davydov, his friend and drinking companion. Rezanov's German physician, George H. von Langsdorff, who was among the ship's company, left a detailed account of the voyage.

The *Juno* navigated the hazardous route down the coast of North America and thirty-two days later entered the harbor of San Francisco. The Spaniards watched the ship from the Presidio with no little apprehension, which did not diminish when Rezanov landed with his sullen and scurvy crew. But it was not long before the Russian won the confidence of the Spanish officials and became a welcome visitor at the house of the San Francisco commandant, Don José Dario Arguello.

There were thirteen children in the Arguello family. One of the girls, sixteen-year-old Concepción, was the belle of the Presidio. Von Langsdorff described her in his memoirs:

> She was lively and animated, had sparkling love-inspiring eyes, beautiful teeth, pleasing and expressive features, a fine form, and a thousand other charms, yet her manners were perfectly simple and artless. Beauties of this kind are to be found, though not frequently, in Italy, Spain, and Portugal.*

Concepción, or Concha as her family called her, and Rezanov were immediately attracted to each other. Von Langsdorff reports:

* George H. von Langsdorff, *Voyages and Travels in Various Parts of the World During the Years 1803, 1804, 1805, 1806, 1807.* Reprint of the 1814 edition (New York: De Capo Press, 1968), p. 153.

The bright eyes of Donna Concepción had made a deep impression upon [Rezanov's] heart; and he conceived that a nuptial union with the daughter of the Commandant at St. Francisco would be a vast step gained towards promoting the political objects he had so much at heart.†

These "political objects" were the overthrow of the Spanish rule and Russian annexation of the Pacific Coast of North America. More than that:

It was forty years before the United States was strong enough to take possession of California, and it is possible that the towering ambition of Rezanov would have acknowledged no bounds short of the Rocky Mountains.‡

Concha eagerly accepted the Russian's proposal with its promise of glittering life at the Imperial Court in St. Petersburg, but her parents would not agree to the union. They were appalled by the thought that their daughter would be marrying outside the faith and feared political complications at the highest levels. But Concha was determined: she pleaded and argued until finally her parents yielded and gave their blessing. The couple were secretly betrothed according to the Roman Catholic rite, though marriage had to await Papal consent and the approval of the Tsar and the King of Spain.

The romance lasted only six weeks, as Rezanov had to start on his long journey to the coast of Siberia, by way of Sitka, and thence overland to St. Petersburg. In the capital he was to obtain the necessary letters from Alexander I to the Pope and the King of Spain, and to arrange the ratification of commercial treaties between Russia and the Spanish colonies in North America. Within two years he hoped to return to California to claim his bride and to realize his political ambitions. Concha resigned herself to a long separation from her betrothed.

The eventful year that had just ended did not dull Rezanov's memory of the rebuff he suffered in Japan. Thoughts of retaliation never left him, and plans for a punitive expedition against the offending Japanese gradually matured. Khvostov and Davydov

† Ibid., p. 183.
‡ Atherton, p. 660.

helped lay the plans, and with the audacity of youth urged action. A series of raids on the Japanese settlements on Sakhalin, the Kuriles, and the northern island of Hokkaido would in some measure soothe the Russian Ambassador's bruised self-esteem, but the main purpose of the attacks would be a show of force to back up new demands that Japan open her ports to Russian merchantmen.

On his return to Sitka from San Francisco, Rezanov busied himself with preparations for the crossing of the Pacific. During the previous winter layover in Sitka when the *Juno* was purchased, the Ambassador had made arrangements for the building of a second ship, a tender. Completed in midsummer, it was lightheartedly christened the *Perchance (Avos)*. In August the expedition left port. Davydov, the master of the new ship, set sail for the Kurile Islands; Khvostov, in command of the *Juno* with Rezanov on board, proceeded to Okhotsk, the starting point of the Ambassador's journey to St. Petersburg across Siberia.

In early October of 1806, Rezanov set off for the capital on horseback. Before leaving he dispatched to Khvostov aboard his ship a set of rather ambiguous instructions for the action against the Japanese.

The raids, most of them carried out the following spring and summer, were successful beyond all expectations. Khvostov and Davydov, with a handful of Russian sailors, performed astonishing deeds of daring and destruction. They overran heavily garrisoned fortifications, razed fishing villages to the ground, attacked and plundered Japanese ships in their own waters, and humiliated the Japanese most painfully by capturing, plundering, and burning one of their war junks, near the port of Hakodate. Loaded to the gunwales with rice, sake, salt, clothing, military supplies, and an endless variety of other goods, the *Juno* and *Perchance* returned to Okhotsk at the end of July. But a strange welcome awaited Khvostov and Davydov: they, their officers, and the ships' crews were promptly arrested and jailed by Captain Bukharin, commandant of Okhotsk. The charge was acting without official orders. The real reason for the arrests was Captain Bukharin's greed. He confiscated—for his own profit—the spoils of the raids, said to have been worth 18,000 rubles.

In jail Khvostov and Davydov were stripped of all but their shoes and clothing, watched constantly by guards with drawn swords, and treated with inhuman harshness. Escape was the only route to survival; they succeeded and eventually made their way to St. Petersburg. The Tsar and Count Rumyantsev, Minister of Commerce, were not inclined to hold them accountable for the raids. But the Admiralty, which reviewed the case at the Tsar's request, thought otherwise. Unexpectedly, the high naval officials exonerated Bukharin and court-martialed Khvostov and Davydov. The young officers, however, escaped punishment. Von Langsdorff explains:

> From their well-known courage, resolution, and professional talents, they were employed in the war against Sweden, in which they distinguished themselves in the command of the gun-boats. Crowned with laurels, they repaired once more to the capital. . . .*

On October 16, 1809, Khovstov and Davydov attended a party at von Langsdorff's St. Petersburg house. The occasion was a reunion with Captain D'Wolf, the former owner of the *Juno,* who had arrived at Kronstadt with a cargo of goods from the United States. After an evening of reminiscences and much good cheer, Khvostov and Davydov set out for their apartments on Vasilevsky Island across the Neva River. Stories of what happened next differ in details, but agree in the main. The drawbridge was open and a ship was passing through. Too impatient to wait, the officers decided to jump onto the vessel and thence to the other side of the bridge. They lost their footing, fell into the river, and were drowned.

Rezanov had met his fate nearly two and a half years earlier. After leaving Okhotsk, he sped toward St. Petersburg, driving himself relentlessly through the frigid Siberian wilderness. Frequently drenched crossing rivers, sleeping in the snow, weakened by the rigors of the past years, he succumbed on March 13, 1807, to a combination of sickness and a fall from a horse. Death caught up with the chamberlain in the small Siberian town of Krasnoyarsk, less than halfway to his destination. He was buried there. Von Langsdorff visited Rezanov's grave in November of 1807 and described it as "a large stone, in the fashion of an altar, but without any inscription."†

* Von Langsdorff, p. 299.
† Von Langsdorff, p. 385.

And Concha? She waited for her bridegroom until she learned of his death, probably in 1816 from the Russians at Fort Ross; then she took the veil, "becoming the first nun in California, Mother Superior of the Dominican convent, St. Catherine of Sienna."‡

‡ Atherton, p. 661.

PART IV

PREFACE TO "VISUAL" POEMS

The depiction of a word is the shadow of its sound. These "visual" poems display the graphic structure of the ideas behind them. As Robert Rauschenberg watched me making lithographs of them, he said that I was trying to produce prints of sounds. In visual poetry the dominant aspect is what Pound called "phanopoiia"— that is, "making manifest." Before the invention of notes, ancient Russian music was written down in the form of "hooks" reminiscent of hieroglyphs. One may also mention in this connection the ancient mime of Eleusis, and modern concrete poetry.

My intention has been to present the *gene* of a poem. In Russia—as also, I am told, in America—the writing of poetry has become a mass phenomenon. Perhaps in the future, poets will have only to provide the gene, or the formula of a poem, leaving it to the reader to improvise whatever he fancies from it.

The interpretation of these visual poems of mine may vary according to the individual temperament. The first one, for example, could be seen as the eternal circle of life—the birth of a brief life from darkness (*tma* in Russian) and its return back to darkness.

The second shows a sea gull. God is invisible but we may guess at the whole of his form from his "bathing trunks"—a sea gull hovering in the sky. This same image is conveyed by more ordinary means in my poem *Public Beach No. 2,* but in the visual poem it is probably expressed with greater precision.

In the third poem, the Russian words MHE TECHO offer a

partial mirror image of the English words ECHO WHEN. An echo is limitless, but when you hear it, you feel all the limits placed on human life, you feel hemmed in, confined—which is the meaning of the Russian MHE TECHO.

The fourth poem consists of the Russian words *a luna kanula*— literally, "the moon has vanished." The words can be read from left to right or from right to left—they form a palindrome. The moment Armstrong made his footprint on the moon, the moon vanished as a symbol of romantic unattainability. Apollo now flies to the moon from left to right, and back again to the earth from right to left. . . .

But once again I must emphasize that these are only surface interpretations of the meanings of the poems.

чайка в к и Б о г а

плачу

ECHO WHEN

ECHO MHE

TECHO

PART V

NOTES

The Russian originals of most of the poems in this volume have been published in two major collections: *Dubovy list violonchelny* (Moscow, 1975) and *Vitrazhnykh del master* (Moscow, 1976), but it should be noted that many poems first appeared in literary periodicals such as *Novy mir, Yunost,* and *Moskva,* in the almanack *Den poezii,* or in *Literaturnaya gazeta.* There are occasionally textual differences between the versions as already published, and, in one or two cases, between them and the texts as published here. (The titles of the two major collections will be abbreviated below as *DLV* and *VDM* respectively.)

I

Nostalgia for the Present: From *VDM.* In Russian the word *nastoyaschee* means not only "present," but also "real," "genuine," or "authentic." This second meaning is perhaps the more important one in the general context of the poem.

Family Graveyard: Written in Dumbarton, Massachusetts, at the grave of Robert Lowell soon after Voznesensky's arrival in the United States in 1977, and first published in English translation in the New York *Times* of October 15, 1977.

In the summer of 1977, a few months before his death, Lowell had visited the house and grave of Pasternak in Peredelkino, near Moscow, and also the little wooden house in Kolomenskoye, on the outskirts of the city, in which Peter the Great once lived.

In the first stanza there is a reference to Lowell's habit of holding his head shyly to one side, in a way reminiscent of a violinist pressing his instrument to his shoulder.

When he visited Lowell's grave, Voznesensky placed on it a branch he had cut from a rowan tree growing next to Pasternak's house in

Peredelkino. In Russia the rowan tree, with its bright red berries (generally seen against a background of snow in winter), is a symbol of life in death, or of resurrection—as in Chapter 12 of Pasternak's *Doctor Zhivago*.

Saga: From *Literaturnaya gazeta,* May 25, 1977.

Table Manners: From *DLV.* Voznesensky has a special interest in music and sometimes recites his verse to a musical accompaniment—as, for example, in his *Poetorio* (written in collaboration with the composer Shchedrin), in which he declaims his verse against the background of an orchestra, a choir, and the singing of ancient Russian dirges. The *Poetorio* has been performed several times in the Moscow Conservatory.

Chagall's Cornflowers: From *DLV.*

This poem was written in 1973, at the time of Marc Chagall's first journey back to his native country since his emigration in 1922. At his poetry readings Voznesensky has described how tears came to Chagall's eyes when he was presented with a bouquet of cornflowers during a visit to Peredelkino, the village near Moscow where many Soviet writers have houses. The flowers reminded Chagall of his childhood in Vitebsk.

Voznesensky has been sharply criticized for this poem in the Soviet press. One critic, Yuri Seleznev, writing in *Almanakh poezii* in 1977, mentioned in a footnote that Chagall had decorated the ceiling of the Knesset in Jerusalem—thus implying that it was inappropriate for Voznesensky to speak in praise of an artist with such clearly expressed "Zionist" sympathies. Chagall drew an illustration to Voznesensky's *The Call of the Lake* (translated by Stanley Kunitz in *Antiworlds and the Fifth Ace*) which describes how the site of a massacre of Jews by the Nazis in World War II has been converted into an amusement park.

"man lives by sky alone": The biblical allusion is clearer in the Russian original, where *nebom* ("by sky") rhymes with *khlebom* ("by bread").

"your canvases rolled up in a tube": Evidently an allusion to the fact that very little of Chagall's work is exhibited in the Soviet Union. Most of his paintings, such as those in the Russian Museum in Leningrad, are still "rolled up in a tube" and stored away out of sight.

O Suzdal Mother of God: From *DLV* (the last line and date have been omitted).

The icon of the Virgin Mary in the old Russian city of Suzdal is one of the most famous.

Provincial Scene: From *Yunost,* July 1977.

"a sweet southern town" (*siropny gorod*): The reference here is evidently to Simferopol, a resort town in the Crimea, where in 1977, with much local publicity, a schoolboy was put on trial for the murder of his mother, a waitress, by the name of Indulskaya, whose body he threw into a privy.

"Bubbles from the earth": A line apparently suggested by Shakespeare's "The earth hath bubbles . . ." (*Macbeth,* Act I, Scene 3).

Alexei Gavrilovich Venetsianov (1780–1847): Russian painter noted for his portraits of Russian peasant women.

The Interment of Nikolia Vasilich Gogol: From *DLV* (with the omission of several stanzas).

There is a story that when Gogol's coffin was opened in order to transfer his remains to another place, it was discovered that he was lying on his side. This poem aroused controversy in the Soviet press—in January 1976 it was attacked in *Zvezda* by Igor Zlatouski, as "libel" on Russian history and literature—but it was defended by Boris Slutski (in *Yunost*) and by Vladimir Soloukhin (in *Literaturnaya gazeta*).

Phone Booth: From *DLV.*

An Arrow in the Wall: From *DLV.*

Do Not Return to Your Old Loves: From *DLV.*

Old Song: From *DLV*, but first published in Bulgarian translation in the Sofia newspaper *Literaturen front* (September 1968), with a dedication to the Bulgarian poet Georgi Dzhagarov.

Anguish: From *DLV.*

On the Death of Shukshin: From *VDM.*

Vasili Makarovich Shukshin (1929–74): A popular prose writer distinguished by his bold and candid approach to his themes, who was also an actor. His most celebrated film was *Kalina krasnaya,* where he played the lead part of a man who had returned from prison, and who dies dramatically on the screen after being stabbed. In another film, *The Lake,* he played the part of someone involved in attempts to save Lake Baikal from pollution—an issue that stirred considerable public concern in the Soviet Union a few years ago in connection with a proposal to build a paper factory on the shore of the lake. Shukshin's premature death (from a heart attack while making a new film) caused widespread grief, and his grave in Novodevichi Monastery, Moscow, attracts a constant flow of visitors.

china ik: A slang word for a cigarette butt.

Serving Time: From *VDM.*

As Voznesensky has explained during his readings, this poem was written after a meeting at the Crimean Observatory with Nikolai Aleksandrovich Kozyrev, a well-known astrophysicist, and the author of an audacious theory according to which time has its own field of gravity. Kozyrev—as is mentioned in Solzhenitsyn's *Archipelago Gulag*—served a sentence in a forced labor camp under Stalin. The fact of his imprisonment is indicated in the poem by an ironical use of the term "State Prize" (formerly known as the "Stalin Prize") "awarded" to him in the repressive years before the war—hence, in the English version, "laureled and locked up in those prewar days."

In recent years time has been an important theme in Voznesensky's poetry, and he has been influenced, as he explains during his poetry readings, not only by Kozyrev's theory, but also by the ideas of the biophysicist Alexander Chizhevsky. (Alexander Leonidovich Chizhevsky, 1897–1964, caused controversy in the mid-twenties by a book on the "physical factors in the biological process" in which he claimed that there is a connection between solar energy and historical events, such as wars and revolutions. He believed that the periodical appearance of men of genius and of great works of art was also conditioned by variations in solar energy. Although he was publicly defended by Tsiolkovsky, the founder of Russian space science, Chizhevsky was denounced at the time as a "sun-worshiper" and "reactionary." At the international convention of astrophysicists in New

261

York in 1939 he was elected in absentia an honorary president and proposed as a candidate for the Nobel Prize, but by this time he had been arrested, and he returned from imprisonment only after Stalin's death, when he was able to resume his academic career. His posthumously published book "The Whole of Life" [*Vaya zhizn*], was published in Moscow in 1974 with a preface by the Soviet cosmonaut Vitali Sevastyanov. A number of Chizhevsky's pupils, now working at the Crimean Observatory, are continuing to develop his theories linking biological rhythms and historical events with solar energy.)

An Ironical Elegy . . . : From *DLV*.

Otorva: Slang for "whore."

Monologue of the World's Last Poetry Reader: From *VDM*.

"huge sports arena": The Luzhniki Stadium in Moscow (mentioned by name in the Russian text) is often used for mass poetry readings.

Smurnov: This is evidently a slightly disguised form of the common name "Smirnov" and may well refer to a contemporary poet, Sergei Vasilyevich Smirnov, who is known for his "orthodox" views and stands here for the army of conventional and not always overtalented poets alluded to in the final stanza of the preceding poem.

The labels on Soviet mineral water bottles commonly depict an eagle about to take flight.

The last stanza is a paraphrase of Pushkin's *Exegi Monumentum* (1836).

War: From *VDM*.

Prayer: From *VDM*, where it is entitled *Michelangelo's Prayer*.

Picture Gallery: From *DLV*.

Winter at the Track: From *DLV*.

The poem is dedicated to Voznesensky's friend Vasili Pavlovich Aksyonov (1932–   ), a novelist and playwright. Aksyonov was together with Voznesensky on the notorious occasion (March 7, 1963) when, at a crowded meeting between members of the government and representatives of the intelligentsia in the Sverdlov Hall of the Kremlin, Khrushchev lost his temper and berated the young writers present in violent language. For about half an hour Khrushchev shook his fist at Voznesensky, angrily accusing him of "formalism," and of wanting to bring about a "Hungarian Revolution" in Russia. Finally, addressing the poet as "Mr. Voznesensky," Khrushchev said, "Clear out of my country—I will tell Shelepin here to give you a passport." At this point Shelepin (who was then the deputy prime minister) got up and shouted at Voznesensky, "How dare you come to the Kremlin without a white shirt, dressed in a sweater like a beatnik?!" When Voznesensky tried to reply, saying that he was a Russian poet and would not leave the country, many of those present in the hall chanted in chorus, "Shame! Down with him!" For a long time after this incident Voznesensky was not allowed to publish anything.

There are several slang terms in the poem: *vynyukhat konyushnyu* means "get a hot tip"; *khanurik* is a current word for an alcoholic.

Do Not Forget: From *VDM*.

"COUNTRY FIRST": In the Russian original, the button reads *GTO,* standing for *Gotov k Trudu i Oborone* ("Ready for Labor and Defense"), a slogan of Soviet youth organizations.

Public Beach No. 2: From *DLV*.

A Chorus of Nymphs: From *DLV* (a section of the long poem entitled *Queen of Clubs,* with the addition of extra lines in this version).

Maya Plisetskaya: Famous ballerina.

Taganka: The theater on the Taganka founded by Yuri Lyubimov and noted for its bold, avant-garde productions—such as the stage version of Voznesensky's *Antiworlds,* which has been put on many times. (Another Voznesensky production, *Save Your Faces,* was banned after the second performance.)

"Rimskaya becomes Korsakova": These names, more familiar to a Western reader, have been substituted for the original "Borisova and Musatova." (Borisov-Musatov was a Russian painter. The two parts of his name have been separated and put in the feminine form in an allusion to the habit of exchanging places while standing in line.)

Ilya Glazunov: A fashionable Moscow painter who specializes in portraits.

The "Gioconda" was recently brought to Moscow, where it was exhibited for a brief period—those who stood in line to see it were allowed to look only for a few moments.

The Feast. From *VDM*.

Written for children, this is one of several poems by Voznesensky on the theme of ecology.

Technology: From *DLV*. (Originally published in the Byelorussian journal *Neman*.)

"a hockey game on TV": The original names two popular stars of Soviet hockey, Kharlamov and Petrov.

"the basis of the family, private property, and the state": There is an allusion here to a work by Friedrich Engels that is required reading in Soviet courses on Marxism.

"synthetic caviar": Soviet scientists recently announced the discovery of a process for making a substitute for the natural product, which in recent years has become scarce through the building of hydroelectric dams on the Volga, and other factors.

Black Buffoonery: From *VDM*.

Mikalojus Chiurlionis (1875–1911): A Lithuanian pioneer of abstract art. Formerly under a ban in the Soviet Union, his work is now exhibited in Kaunas.

The Eternal Question: From *DLV*.

II

Requiem: From *VDM*.

June '68: From *VDM*.

Sergei Yesenin (1895–1925): Famous Russian poet who in one well-known photograph bears a striking resemblance to John F. Kennedy. (In Voznesensky's play *Save Your Faces,* referred to above, the actors at one point carried portraits of both Kennedy and Yesenin.)

"the roots of apple trees": In introducing this poem Voznesensky mentions that in the spring of 1967, while dining with Lowell and others at the New York apartment of the President's widow, he was struck by the apple trees in blossom on the balcony.

Lines to Robert Lowell: From *VDM.*

San Francisco Is Kolomenskoye: From *Ten' Zvuka* (1970).

The Church of the Ascension, which stands on a hill in Kolomenskoye near Moscow, is famous for its great height, its unrelieved whiteness, and its single steeple.

From a Diary: Written during a visit to the United States in 1977. In his readings Voznesensky says this is a pendant to his poem *Avos*—as though from the diary of a latter-day Rezanov (see *Story Under Full Sail*).

Dogalypse: From *DLV.*

The poem refers to an occasion when Voznesensky read his poetry at the Simon Frazer University, Vancouver (together with Lawrence Ferlinghetti and Robert Bly). Many of the students who attended brought dogs and other pets (including a raccoon) with them.

Halloween Apples: First published in English translation in the New York *Times.*

In Russian, under the title *Yabloki s britvami* ("Apples with Razor Blades") in *VDM.* The incident described actually took place.

Striptease on Strike: From *DLV.*

Long Island Beach: Written during the poet's visit to the United States in 1977.

American Buttons: From *VDM.*

Sources: Written during the poet's visit to Berkeley in 1971, this is one of several responses to accusations of "pornography" from Soviet critics.

Silent Tingling: From *VDM.*

(The translation is from the original version, written in Australia, March 1972.)

A Boat on the Shore: From *DLV.*

Christmas Beaches: From *DLV.*

Lazha is a current slang word for "nonsense."

Mudrily is a slightly disguised form of *mudily* (i.e., not from *mudry,* "wise," but from *mudi,* "balls"—*mudit'* means to talk boring nonsense, and *mudily* can be translated as "bores").

"Don't cry. This isn't 'Prince Igor'": Reference to the scene in Borodin's opera, when Prince Igor's wife, Yaroslavna, weeps on the walls of Putivl.

Ant: From *DLV.*

Breath Donor: From *DLV.*

At the Glass-blowing Factory: From *VDM.*

Ninel: a girl's name formed from "Lenin," spelled backwards.

Baikonur: the Soviet equivalent of Cape Canaveral.

Snowdrops: From *DLV.*

Kemar'te from *kemarit',* a slang word for "sleep."

Shame: From the text as published in *DLV.* The poem was first recited by Voznesensky in the Taganka Theater in 1968, not long after he had protested in an angry letter to *Pravda* about the Soviet authorities' refusal to allow him to visit America for a poetry reading to which he had been invited there. The letter was not, needless to say, published by *Pravda*, but it appeared shortly afterward in French translation in *Le Monde*. In the version of the poem as read from the stage of the Taganka, which then circulated widely in Moscow in handwritten copies, there is a stanza—never published in the Soviet Union—that seems to refer to the persistent rumors that Mikhail Sholokhov, the author of the Soviet classic *The Silent Don*, may have been a plagiarist or had an unacknowledged co-author:

> *Sverkhklassik i satrap,*
> *Stydites, dorogoi—*
> *Odin roman sodral,*
> *Ne smog sodrat' vtoroi.*
> ("Superclassic and satrap,
>   Shame on you, dear fellow—
>   You stole one novel,
>   But were unable to steal a second one.")

skhokhmin (from the noun *khokhma,* a joke or wisecrack): "tell jokes," a slang word borrowed from Yiddish.

Dry Spell: From *VDM.*

The Edge: From *DLV.*

The Russian Intelligentsia: From *VDM* (with the omission of stanzas 5 and 6).

For Kozyrev, see the note on *Serving Time.*

Sviatoslav Richter (1914–   ): Famous pianist. Sergei Averintsev: Literary scholar and historian, lecturer at Moscow University.

Pornography of the Mind: From *DLV* (with omission of stanzas 4, 6, 7, and 8). Like *Sources,* a response to accusations of "pornography."

"short-order cook": The Russian word here, *stryapukha,* is bound to remind Russian readers of a play so entitled by Anatoli Sofronov (1911–70), the editor of the popular illustrated weekly *Ogoniok* and a writer of conservative views who played a part in the anti-Semitic campaign of the late Stalin years.

"secret millionaires": People who have made fortunes from black-marketeering or embezzlement of state enterprises.

Ice Block: From *DLV.* The final section of a long poem, first published in *Yunost* under the title *Ice–69.*

As Voznesensky has explained at readings of the poem, it was written under the impact of the tragic death of a student of Moscow University, Svetlana Popova, who became trapped in a snowbank while skiing with a companion. The other people out skiing at the same time did not bother to look for them, and Svetlana froze to death. Her companion, who survived, later described how, in order to keep up their spirits, she recited from memory poems from Voznesensky's *Antiworlds.* Voznesensky learned these details in a letter from the girl's father after her death (the letter is published, together with the poem, in *Yunost*).

"You wretched pack of toadies . . ." (*Vy, zhalkoyu tolpoyu . . .*): This and the following lines are a paraphrase of Lermontov's *On the Death of a Poet* (1837), an impassioned denunciation of the timeservers through whose machinations Pushkin was killed in a duel.

Darkmotherscream: From *DLV*.

Skrymtymnym is a word used by folk singers in the Omsk region of Siberia. (The inhabitants of Omsk are called *omichi*.) The word, chanted as a refrain, is of obscure—perhaps shamanistic—origin and has no precisely definable meaning, but to a Russian ear it has a number of phonetic associations with other words, such as those for "hidden," "darkness," and "prison."

Yelabuga: Town on the river Kama, where in 1941, the great Russian poet Marina Tsvetayeva hanged herself.

Shagadam, magadam: Also, apparently, shamanistic words. (Shamans are Siberian witch doctors.) The second of them inevitably evokes for a Russian reader the name Magadan—a town in the remote far eastern part of Siberia that was notorious in Stalin's time for the forced labor camps where countless prisoners died of cold and hunger.

Star: From *VDM*.

Naked Goddess, Apparently an allusion to the "Silver Nymph" award made at a French film festival to the actress Tatyana Lavrova, to whom the poem is addressed.

Elegy Written in the Little House of Ovid: From *Literaturnaya gazeta,* May 25, 1977.

The Lake: From *VDM*.

Stanza 8 refers to an accident in 1970, when Voznesensky was being driven in a car near Alma-Ata by the Kazakh poet Olzhas Suleymanov. (The accident is described at length in a poem published in the collection *Vzglyad* [Moscow, 1973].)

Book Boom: Published here for the first time.

In the years until Stalin's death, Anna Akhmatova (1889–1966) was persecuted and her work was banned. A recent volume of her verse, published in an edition of 200,000 copies, was sold out immediately, and is now obtainable only on the black market—an ironic comment on the frequent assertion in Stalin's time that she was a poet who had written only for a decadent, prerevolutionary elite and was of no interest to Soviet readers.

"Massivy Muravlev" (in the Russian original only): An invented name, but, judging from the suggestive use of the word "crane" (*zhuravl'* in Russian) in the same stanza, it may have been suggested by that of a poet called Zhuravlev.

The Beaver's Lament: From *DLV*.

According to Voznesensky's commentary on the poem during readings, it was inspired by an actual event that happened in Byelorussia: a colony of beavers, whose habitation was about to be destroyed by bulldozers, came out to defend it and were seen to be weeping tears.

III

Page, 207, lines 6 and 8: In these names the accent falls on the second syllable—Rezánov, Khvostóv, Davýdov. In the Russian text of the poem, the names of the two officers are spelled Khvastov and Dovydov, although in the prose passages the names appear in their historical form.

Page 207, line 9: The name of the second ship in Russian is *Avos*. The word is an expression of hope where chances of success appear slim. It may be translated as "perchance," "perhaps," "maybe," "on the off-chance."

Page 211, lines 7 and 8: Ltierally translated, the lines read, "On dry land corvée and Fonvizins,/but we have a springtime motto, 'Perchance!'" Here the poet speaks of serfdom in Russia, of conformist neoclassic writers, but proclaims, "We have faith in freedom!"

Page 211, line 13: This echoes a poem by Pasternak, "We are few./ Three, perhaps, altogether," and Voznesensky's own poem to Akhmadulina, "We are many./Four, perhaps, altogether."

Page 213, line 27: In the original this is a play on words—*avos* (perchance) and A. Voz(nesensky).

Page 215, lines 2–4: The reference is to the twelfth-century Russian epic *The Song of Igor's Campaign*. Yaroslavna, wife of Igor, bemoans her husband's wounds suffered in a battle with the Kumans, a warlike Turkic tribe of nomads. Konchakovna, daughter of a Kuman chieftain, Konchak, married Vladimir, son of Igor, whom the Kumans had captured. A year later Vladimir was released and Konchakovna returned with her husband to his native town.

Page 217, line 1: Rezanov's Prayer has more than a casual relation to Voznesensky's highly personal poem "A Seafarer's Confession," *Novy Mir*, No. 9 (1971), p. 104, in which the line "Well, what more do you want from me?" also dominates.

Page 217, line 6: Here the poet speaks of his own origins—not Rezanov's.

Page 221, line 4: In the original "a Nehru jacket" is *bitlovka*, a Russian slang expression that derives from "Beatles" and describes a style of shirt with a standing collar popularized by the famous rock group.

Page 223, line 1: Dmitriev, Ivan Ivanovich (1760–1837), Russian poet, fabulist, and satirist.

Page 223, line 7: Stainislavskly used to say, "Theater begins in the cloakroom," that is, the public should be prepared for the experience from the moment it enters the theater.

Page 229, line 25: Golovnin, Vasily Mikhailovich (1776–1831), Russian naval officer and explorer who sailed the North Pacific in the years immediately following Rezanov's visits to Japan and North America.

Page 231, line 7: Derzhavin, Gavrila Romanovich (1743–1816), Russian poet, statesman, at one time Secretary to Catherine the Great.

Page 231, line 9: "I built myself a rare and lasting monument" is the first line of the poem "A Monument" by Derzhavin, originally titled "To the Muse. After Horace." There is a tradition among Russian poets to return to Horace's poem "A Monument" and recast the idea according to their own artistic credo.

Voznesensky's "monument" has this meaning: the poet insults his contemporaries and the future generations by telling them that they have no art. Angry, just to prove him wrong, they create superb art—a monument to the poet.

Page 235, line 22: The Mother of God gave Rezanov a medallion with her autograph—a token of love.

Page 205, line 12: Avvakum (1620 or 1621–82), Russian Orthodox priest, leader of the Old Believers, who refused to recognize the reforms introduced by the official Church in the middle of the seventeenth century. He was a famous polemicist, a master of invective and the condemnatory statement.